Paddle Steamers

PRINCESS ELIZABETH

David L. Williams

Ian Allan
PUBLISHING

Front cover:
Decked out in the new
Wightlink colours, the *Ryde*
arrives off Ryde pierhead in
September 1968.
John Edgington

Back cover:
Berthed in the harbour at
Weymouth on 30 September
1962, the 66-year-old Cosens
paddle pleasure steamer
Consul. R. C. Riley

Title page:
The last Red Funnel paddle
steamer, the *Princess Elizabeth*,
on 25 June 1957,
approaching Ryde Pier, Isle of
Wight. The *Princess Elizabeth*
was converted from coal- to
oil-burning in 1946, after her
return from war service.
R. C. Riley

CONTENTS

Bibliography

ADAMS, R. B., *Red Funnel and Before*
ARCHBOLD, Michael, *Red Funnel — A Pictorial History*
COLLARD, Chris,
   P. & A. Campbell Pleasure Steamers 1887-1945
   P. & A. Campbell Pleasure Steamers from 1946
HANCOCK, H. E., *Semper Fidelis — The Story of the Navvies*
HOCKING, Charles, *Disasters at Sea during the Age of Steam*
LENTON, H. T., and COLLEDGE, J. J., *Warships of World War II*
McCRORIE, Ian, *Clyde Pleasure Steamers — An Illustrated History*
THOMAS, John, *British Railways Steamers of the Clyde*
THOMPSON, A. G., *The Thames — And All That, 1824-1935*
WILLIAMS, David L., *White's of Cowes*
WINCHESTER, Clarence, *Shipping Wonders of the World*
WINSER, John de S., *BEF Ships before, at and after Dunkirk*
Reference was also made to the Tramscape Historical Database and
Tom Lee websites of paddle-steamer resources.

Acknowledgements

I should like to thank the following persons and organisations
for the help they gave to me in the preparation of this book:
Gibbie Anderson (Clyde River Steamers Club)
Shirley Anderson (Red Funnel Group)
Tony Butler (Cowes Maritime Museum)
Douglas Champion
Ken Crowe (Southend-on-Sea Borough Council)
John Edgington
Imperial War Museum
Tom Lee
John Megoran (Paddle Steamer Preservation Society)
Bert Moody – for all of the steamer posters
Emma Morgan
Stephen Rabson (P&O Steam Navigation Co)
David Reed (Isle of Wight branch of the World Ship Society)
Dick Riley
the late Ray Sprake
Gordon Stewart (Tramscape)
Mike Tozer
Adrian Vicary (Maritime Photo Library)
the late Kenneth Wightman
Rachel Wragg (Southampton City Council Cultural Services)
World Ship Society

First published 2002

ISBN 0 7110 2772 2

Published by Ian Allan Publishing

an imprint of Ian Allan Publishing Ltd,
Hersham, Surrey KT12 4RG.

Printed by Ian Allan Printing Ltd, Hersham, Surrey KT12 4RG.

Code: 0202/B2

INTRODUCTION

In the collective imagination, paddle steamers rank alongside steam locomotives, flying boats and other vintage vehicle types as symbols of a more elegant style of transportation from a bygone era. They represent a period in time when the pace of life was more sedate, a time when people generally were less sophisticated and more content with the simple pleasures of life. And because, today, there is a strong yearning for some of those values, if not for the drudgery and toil of life prior to electronic tools and utensils, so it amplifies the nostalgia for paddle steamers and memories of summer excursions from pier heads all around the United Kingdom.

Paddle propulsion takes us back to the very dawn of powered navigation. From the very first steam-engined ships of the early 1800s, it remained the dominant form of propulsion on ocean-crossing vessels until the third quarter of the 19th century and, for coastal services and harbour towage, held on for another 75 or so years.

The great benefit of a sturdy paddle wheel on either side of a ship, compared with submerged screw propellers located aft, was greater manœuvrability, particularly at slow speeds and in shallow water. Until reversing gears were developed and, much later, variable-pitch propellers and bow and stern thrusters, the excellent handling characteristics of twin paddle wheels ensured their supremacy over the screw propeller, other than for deep-water trading.

The coastal paddle steamer established itself in three distinct forms of passenger-carrying operation: scheduled service work around the British coast, excursion cruises and, uniquely, at the Port of Southampton, tendering the great liners that did not complete the run from the Solent up Southampton Water to the docks.

Scheduled services, providing an unrivalled standard of reliable public transport for their time, were operated in certain regions all year round as part of an emerging national public transport system led by the railways. A variety of routes was established, in the Thames Estuary, along the River Clyde, between North Devon and South Wales and linking the Isle of Wight to the mainland, as well as elsewhere.

The expansion of the railway system in the Victorian age opened up not only a true public transport system in Great Britain; in effect, it also created another new 'industry' — tourism. By the end of the 19th century, where once there had been only tiny coastal villages, whole towns had grown up to cater for what was rapidly becoming a national fashion — the seaside holiday. The essential ingredients of this sweeping social change were the railway links which permitted the movement of large numbers of people from the cities and inland towns to the coast.

Just as the spas and seaside resorts owed their growth in popularity to the railways, in turn they stimulated the development of other forms of transport to extend the recreation of holidaymakers, notable among them being coastal pleasure steamers. So the many small paddle steamers already being used as a means of regular transport, itself usually swollen by the increased summer traffic, were diverted to pleasure trips as an equally valuable source of revenue. As such, they were the precursors of other, later forms of mass leisure transport such as charabanc and coach tours and ocean-liner cruises.

Off-peak and, later, almost all-year-round cruising developed from the regular passenger work, offering holidaymakers a welcome break from strolling the promenade or dozing in a deckchair. They took trippers to local places of interest or sightseeing in the great ports or on special excursions, such as to observe the Fleet Reviews. Taking advantage of the chain of Victorian seaside piers that developed in parallel, the coastal paddle excursion soon became an integral feature of the British seaside holiday scene, and the subsequent evolution of the coastal paddle steamer owed as much to this focus on entertainment as to anything else.

In Scotland, on the Clyde, it was a trip 'doon the watter'. On the Thames and the East Coast, they were the 'butterfly-boats', fluttering their little paddle wings as they busily nosed in

The *Waverley* leaving Ryde pier at the time of her first trip to the Isle of Wight.
David Reed — 01517

The *Queen of the South* (ex-*Jeanie Deans*) ran a short season of pleasure cruises in 1967 for the Coastal Steam Packet Co. Replicating the old Eagle Line services, she operated from Tower Pier and Greenwich to Southend-on-Sea and Herne Bay.

▲ and out of pier heads in the height of the season in a seemingly constant rotation. It was the same in the West Country, along the North Wales Coast and around the Isle of Wight.

▶▶ The vessels themselves were invariably magnificent, brightly painted and comfortably furnished and appointed, though often open to the weather. They were capable of high speeds and were extraordinarily reliable, the relative simplicity of the machinery driving their side paddle wheels no doubt having a bearing on this. That said, there was the occasional mishap, as will be discovered.

These wonderful, charismatic little steamers were also given magical names, of heroes and heroines, of celebrities and romantic places, all of which gave the public imagination much to conjure with. There were the *Lorna Doone*, *Ivanhoe*, *Maid of the Loch*, *Iona*, *Westward Ho*, *Jeanie Deans*, *Gracie Fields* and *Balmoral*, to name just a few. Some companies followed distinct naming styles by which their services and ships could be readily identified: for example, there were the 'Belle' steamers of the Essex coast, the 'Queens' of the Medway and General Steam Navigation's 'Eagle' boats.

In the late Victorian era, paddle-steamer services were run by a large number of private operators. To get a share of the

business, the railway companies also began to establish shipping divisions. Gradually, from around the beginning of the 20th century, these operating companies began to combine together. As a result, after a time, particular operators became associated with only certain operating regions. The railway companies quickly strengthened their steamer operations, both on coastal and short sea routes, while they too were increasingly amalgamating into bigger concerns, so that, when the great reorganisation of the railways into four major operating companies occurred in 1923, the number of paddle-ship owners reduced yet further.

Despite the thinning-down of the rival concerns, paddle-ship services and excursion trips remained as popular as ever. If anything, their popularity increased between the two World Wars. Thus the early 20th century and, in particular, the period from 1920 into the 1950s is remembered as the paddle steamer's heyday.

By the late 1950s the paddle steamer was already competing with diesel- or turbine-powered screw vessels, and as fundamental changes to social habits gathered momentum and emerging trends in new forms of mass travel dictated a requirement for a quite different type of coastal passenger craft — the Ro-Ro car ferry — so the numbers of paddle steamers began to decline. This reversal of fortunes was accelerated by major changes in holidaymaking preferences. Within a very short period of time, the package holiday on the Costa del wherever, with its guaranteed sunshine, and made affordable by cheaper air fares, began to take over.

At the same time, many of the coastal piers, no longer patronised as they once were, fell into disrepair, in some cases leading to their complete demolition and removal. It is a salutary reinforcement of this point to consider that the Isle of Wight alone, which once had more than 10 piers, today has only half that number. Just as you cannot run trains without stations and tracks, so it becomes difficult, if not impossible, to run steamer services, especially excursions, without piers.

Thus the remaining paddle-steamer services fell away rapidly in the 1950s and 1960s, with the very last scheduled service run by the *Lincoln Castle* in 1977 across the River Humber from New Holland to Hull. No new coastal paddle vessels had been constructed since the *Maid of the Loch*, which entered service in

The *Queen of the South*, the former *Jeanie Deans*, off Gravesend in January 1966. Her new owners repainted her in North British Railway colours, which, with her wooden enclosed bridge, gave her an attractive, vintage look.
Kenneth Wightman

PADDLE STEAMER
QUEEN OF THE SOUTH
SUMMER SEASON '67
Commencing Saturday June 10

LONDON-SOUTHEND, KENT & ESSEX COASTS
daily service
(EXCEPT FRIDAY)

also delightful evening cruises on
Thursdays, Saturdays and Sundays.
(Commencing Saturday June 17)

EARLY BOOKINGS STRONGLY ADVISED

A. E. MARTIN & CO. LTD. Managers for
COASTAL STEAM
PACKET CO. LTD.
52-53 Crutched Friars, City of London, E.C.3.
Tel: ROYAL 0281-4 Telex: 22472
Booking Office — Sailings from SOUTHEND only —
Pier Approach. Tel: SOUTHEND 67505

1953 for excursion trips on Loch Lomond. Many of those that still remained were progressively retired and scrapped, while others were diverted to a variety of dubious roles, often secured idle in some river berth somewhere or other, their interiors completely interfered with until they were left almost unrecognisable. Gone were the jolly day-trippers, replaced by a new type of transient occupant only superficially interested in their origins — the 'yuppie' diners of the floating restaurants or the disco-dancers of the quayside nightclubs. Thank goodness that some (at least) of these steamers have been rescued and spared this ignominious fate, to be restored and opened as memorials to the great era of the coastal paddle ship or operated on nostalgic trips as reminders of the past.

Today only two paddle steamers remain in active operation, engaged on a regular season of coastal cruises. They are the twin-funnelled *Waverley*, once of Caledonian Steam Packet ownership, and the former River Dart steamer *Kingswear Castle*, restored by the Paddle Steamer Preservation Society and now making pleasure trips on the Medway. The sight of these vessels making their way around the coast provides an enduring and appealing reminder of those wonderful 'Glory Days' of the coastal paddle steamers — of long, pleasant summer days running from Weston-super-Mare to Ilfracombe, from Prestatyn to Rhyl or from the Medway to Clacton; of heroic deeds off the beaches of Dunkirk in Britain's darkest hour; and of reliable passenger services when cups of tea were drunk from china crockery and the seats you sat on were not made of plastic!

This book is not intended to be a detailed historical record of British coastal paddle steamers, with precise engineering specifications and exactitudes of information on the dates and places when vessels were commissioned, or in which seasons they operated on given routes. Rather, it is, unashamedly, a book of images and descriptions set against an historical background, and intended primarily to evoke the flavour of those smart little steamers in their heyday and the delights of coastal cruises in summers long ago. The pages that follow will, it is hoped, be a constant source of pleasurable nostalgia to those who remember a time of quieter values and gentle contentment.

1. DAWNING OF A GOLDEN AGE — A REVIEW OF COASTAL PADDLE-STEAMER SERVICES 1900-19

The Victorian era witnessed the great flowering of the Industrial Revolution, as it is now known. Huge iron and steel works arose around the country, fuelled by cheap and plentiful coal. Immense shipyards sprang up on the Clyde and the Tyne and at Barrow, Belfast and Birkenhead. Railway lines spread out in a rapidly radiating network like a vast spider's web, and, along the coast, from the various station termini, a myriad of small steam-powered ships conveyed passengers along river estuaries to otherwise inaccessible towns and villages or to offshore islands.

In 1900 the car had barely been invented; there were few proper roads, let alone motorways or other trunk routes suitable for motor vehicles. The first powered flight was still some three years off, and the aeroplane itself would remain an impractical form of mass transportation for another 20 years, at least. For an increasingly mobile public, the only realistic means of travelling anywhere were train or coastal paddle steamer.

Already, by the turn of the century, both rail and coastal steamship services had clocked up over 70 years of operation. Indeed, the coastal passenger ship was not only well established as a regular service ferry but also in the expanding pleasure cruise business. By the late 1800s, nearly every seaside resort around the British coast had a pier with at least one steamer of some sort operating from it. It has been recorded that, by the end of the 19th century, more than 300 steam-powered vessels had already been engaged in passenger service on the Clyde Estuary alone, and the picture was much the same around the rest of the United Kingdom's coastline.

Rivalry was intense too, the lucrative commuter and holiday trades attracting the interest of pure ship operators and railway companies alike. On the Firth of Clyde, where the Scottish railway operators were keen to take advantage of the profitable marine passenger business, their proposals to set up their own steamship services met with Government disapproval. They were not to be thwarted, though, and, as a means of avoiding unfavourable Parliamentary rulings, each established a steamer packet service to operate ships on its behalf as a separate

concern. Thus it was, at the beginning of the 20th century, that three of the region's railway companies had a presence on the Clyde. The Caledonian Steam Packet Co was formed in 1889 by the Caledonian Railway, the Glasgow & South Western Steam Packet Co commenced operations for the Glasgow & South Western Railway in 1891, and the North British Steam Packet Co, which dated back to 1866, represented the North British Railway.

Among the front-line Clyde steamers of the day were the *Jupiter* (1896) and *Juno* (1898), the *Mercury* (1892) and *Caledonia* (1889), North British Railway's classic *Waverley* (1889) and MacBrayne's *Iona* and *Columba*, running the longer-distance routes to the Western Isles.

Further south, the coast from Morecambe Bay out to Anglesey, along the North Wales coastline, was another area of concentrated steamship activity. The many Victorian piers along the 100-mile stretch of coastline made this an ideal centre for pleasure steamer operations as the new holiday resorts blossomed. A range of services extended from Barrow to Morecambe and Blackpool or to Whitehaven, from the Mersey out to the resorts of Llandudno, Rhyl and Prestatyn and, using larger vessels, out to Douglas on the Isle of Man. Though designated as a short-sea rather than a coastal ship, one of the largest paddle steamers to operate in United Kingdom waters up to that time was based in this area. She was the Isle of Man Steam Packet Co's *Empress Queen*. With measurements of 1,995 gross tons and 360ft (109.8m) overall length, she was exceeded in size only by the 2,205-gross-ton former cross-Channel excursion paddle ship *La Marguerite*.

In 1904 the *La Marguerite,* owned by New Palace Steamers, was sold to the Liverpool & North Wales Steamship Co, taking an unsurpassed standard of luxury and spaciousness to the Anglesey service from the Mersey, where she remained for the next 20 years. Other big paddlers in this region, working the Isle of Man routes, included the *Queen Victoria* and the similar *Prince of Wales*.

In the Bristol Channel, the company that would eventually become the dominant paddle-steamer operator was in the

◀◀ Berthed at Rothesay, on the Isle of Bute, the *Mercury* built in 1892 for the Glasgow & South Western Railway.
Ian Allan Library

The Williamson-Buchanan steamer *Isle of Arran* making her way upriver. Her 44-year career, which began on Buchanan Steamers' Glasgow–Arran route, ended in 1936. *Ian Allan Library*

One of the two Loch Lomond steamers operated by the Dumbarton & Balloch Joint Line Committee, the 304-gross-ton *Prince Edward*. The other was the smaller *Princess May*. *Ian Allan Library*

The Clyde paddler *Duchess of Fife*, built in 1903 by Fairfields, not to be confused with the London & South Western Railway vessel of the same name which was built four years earlier and worked the Solent routes (see page 15). *Ian Allan Library*

Built originally for New Palace Steamers' cross-Channel route to Ostend, the *La Marguerite* spent most of her career on the excursion service along the North Wales coast from Liverpool to Llandudno Pier, until withdrawn in 1925. She was the largest paddle steamer ever operated in UK coastal waters. *Simplon Postcards*

process of consolidating its position following the inauguration of services centred on Bristol back in 1889. At that time, the brothers Peter and Alec Campbell, sons of the famous Clyde paddle-ship operator Captain Robert Campbell, had sold their business interests on the Firth of Clyde to the Caledonian Steam Packet Co, which, along with the other railway companies, would soon dominate that trade. By comparison, steamer services on the Bristol Channel were still largely undeveloped and offered good prospects, enticing the Campbell brothers to transfer their operational base.

From that time, the famous White Funnel fleet of P. & A. Campbell was to emerge as one of the leading operators of coastal excursions, a dominant position it was to retain until the 1960s. Services across the Severn Estuary linked Bristol and Weston-super-Mare with the South Wales ports of Cardiff and Newport, as well as the resorts of Barry and Penarth.

The fast paddler *Cambria*, one of a group of three similar steamers, the others being the *Westward Ho* and the *Britannia*. Ian Allan Library

The *Ravenswood*, P. & A. Campbell's earliest paddle steamer specially built for its Bristol Channel services. Beyond her is a famous West Country landmark, the Clifton Suspension Bridge over the Avon Gorge. The Hotwells Landing Stage, which the *Ravenswood* has just left, is on the far side of the bridge, on the left bank. *M. J. Tozer collection*

Marine Excursions for the 1914 season, featuring the *Balmoral* ('The Greyhound of the South'), *Bournemouth Queen* and *Lorna Doone* of White Funnel Steamers and the *Stirling Castle*, *Princess Helena* and other vessels of Red Funnel Steamers.

The Southampton, Isle of Wight and South of England
ROYAL MAIL STEAM PACKET COMPANY, Ltd.

Bournemouth and District.

White Funnel Steamers
'Balmoral,' 'Bournemouth Queen,' 'Lorna Doone,' &c.

From Bournemouth
Cherbourg
July 20th, 1908.
3hrs. 37mins.

From Cherbourg
Bournemouth,
July 20th, 1908.
3hrs. 41mins.

S.S. BALMORAL.—The Greyhound of the South.
Speed 20 Knots.

Red Funnel Steamers
'Stirling Castle,' 'Princess Helena,' &c.

POPULAR MARINE EXCURSIONS
For the Season 1914.

Observer Chambers,
Albert Road, Bournemouth.
T. WILKINS, Manager.
Telephone No. 1134.

Further west, the beautiful coastline of Somerset and North Devon was ideal for sightseeing tours. During the summer season the little steamers ventured down to Minehead, Ilfracombe and Westward Ho!, out to Lundy Island in mid-Channel and to Swansea and the Gower peninsula on the north shore.

A steamship of note, the original *Waverley*, built in 1885, whose name would remain one of distinction among paddlers, was brought south to inaugurate the P. & A. Campbell operations in the Bristol Channel. She was joined in 1891 by the *Ravenswood*, the first of a long line of smart new paddle steamers commissioned by the Campbells for their excursion and packet services. Two groups of three vessels, all built by the Ailsa Shipbuilding Co, soon followed — the sister ships *Westward Ho*, *Cambria* and *Britannia* from 1894 to 1896, and the later sisters *Lady Ismay*, *Glen Avon* and *Glen Usk* between 1911 and 1914.

Although the Campbell brothers had detected a gap in the market that they could exploit, their new-found presence on the Bristol Channel was not without a measure of competition.

River Avon Bristol. 832.

Cosens had some of the oldest vessels on the British register in its fleet. This is the *Premier*, built by Denny in 1846. Her decks are full of naval ratings being conveyed between ship and shore at Devonport, one of the services Cosens provided, which intensified during World War 1. At the time of her disposal, she was the oldest paddle steamer in the UK, and older than any other ship then holding a British BOT certificate.
R. C. Riley collection

The first *Monarch*, one of Cosens' most popular pleasure steamers for over 60 years. *Ian Allan Library*

▲ In 1904 the Barry Railway Co received Parliamentary approval to run steamer services on the Bristol Channel, subject to the condition that they started and finished at Barry Island. The company ordered two magnificent new twin-funnelled

steamers — *Gwalia* and *Devonia* — from John Brown, their deliveries timed to permit commencement of the service in the spring of 1905. They were joined by the *Barry*, also built by John Brown, in 1907.

The Barry Railway, however, sought to increase its passenger volumes by improper means, deviously avoiding the Government-imposed restrictions — practices that brought a swift and resolute reaction from the Campbells. Using all legal means at its disposal, P. & A. Campbell ensured that all operational conditions were enforced against its competitor. This severely limited passenger numbers, such that insufficient revenues were generated even to maintain the ships. From summer 1910 they passed into the ownership of Bristol Channel Passenger Boats, which continued to feel the pinch, until, after just one more season, the fleet was put up for sale yet again. The *Gwalia* went to the Furness Railway as the *Lady Moyra*, but more would be seen of her on the Bristol Channel later. The *Devonia* and *Barry* passed into rival hands, registered with P. & A. Campbell from the 1912 season — another round of opposition effectively dealt with.

The South Devon coastline was characterised by a near absence of seaside piers. As a result, excursion trips and regular services were virtually non-existent in this area. Several attempts were made to establish operations in the region, but the necessity of travelling out and back from either Plymouth or Torquay in the south or around Cornwall from Ilfracombe in quite exposed waters presented difficulties, and profitable sailings could not be sustained. Those ships that were briefly introduced on these routes were obliged to run up on beaches to embark and disembark passengers — a practice that was not without its risks.

The one isolated location of vibrant steamer operations in this part of the country was on the River Dart, on the navigable stretch between Totnes and Dartmouth, for which a particularly distinctive type of small, wooden paddle vessel was developed. This trade was dominated by the River Dart Steamboat Co, formerly the Dartmouth Steam Packet Co, which operated the various 'Castle' steamers.

Along the coast to the east, another major centre of paddle-steamer services had emerged, extending from Weymouth in Dorset through to Brighton in Sussex and beyond. Here, by the start of the 20th century, there were three principal operating companies.

Based at Weymouth was Cosens & Co, the smallest of the three concerns, which operated a fleet of excursion vessels in the season, making trips to Bournemouth, Swanage and the Isle of Wight. Founded in 1845 by Captain Joseph Cosens with the little paddler *Rose*, the fleet was characterised by having some of the oldest vessels on the British register.

Centred on Southampton was the Southampton, Isle of Wight & South of England Royal Mail Steam Packet Co — one of the longest company names ever registered — which later, thankfully, came to be better known as Red Funnel Steamers. Red Funnel ran regular passenger and mail services to Cowes, Isle of Wight, and excursion trips in the summer season to Solent and South Coast resorts, as well as across the Channel.

The London & South Western Railway also ran regular ferry services to the Isle of Wight, between Portsmouth and Ryde and from Lymington to Yarmouth. The vessels based at

P. S. "Lorna Doone".

Portsmouth took advantage of the great warships based in the ▲ naval port as a focus of excursion interest, as well as the occasional naval reviews off Spithead, just as the Red Funnel boats exploited the attraction of the massive liners of the 'transatlantic ferry' entering and leaving Southampton Docks as a feature of their pleasure-cruise programme.

The *Lorna Doone*, one of the most popular and profitable of the excursion steamers operated by the Southampton & Isle of Wight Steam Packet, after her promenade deck had been extended for her full length. *David Reed Collection*

Cowes, Isle of Wight, in the 1906 season, with the *Solent Queen* arriving at the Victoria Pier. Among the first steamers employed by the Southampton & Isle of Wight Royal Mail Steam Packet on pleasure cruises, she was completed in 1889. Her active career lasted until 1948. *Red Funnel Group*

Red Funnel's excursion services extended in an easterly direction as far as the Sussex resorts of Littlehampton, Brighton and Eastbourne. As early as 1897, the Campbells had sought to widen their operations into the South Coast region to complement those services already established at Bristol. However, the Solent proved to be an area of particularly intense and insuperable competition. P. & A. Campbell did not abandon the Solent altogether in the face of such odds, but, recognising that a more attractive opportunity existed further east, the company launched new services from Brighton. Any local opposition was swiftly acquired, and P. & A. Campbell soon established itself as the dominant force in the area, commensurate with its position in the West Country.

The third great area of coastal passenger services and seasonal excursions, fuelled by the demand for pleasure cruises by the population of London and the adjacent counties, was the Thames Estuary, extending from Tower Bridge, in the heart of the capital, out to the resorts of Clacton and Walton-on-the-Naze in Essex and to the Thanet ports of Margate and Ramsgate, in Kent. Feeding into the River Thames, the River Medway in Kent was another centre of excursion services, connecting Strood and Rochester with Southend-on-Sea and other resorts on the Essex coast. These latter services were maintained, virtually unchallenged, by the Medway Steam Packet Co — the Queen Line, as it was popularly known. As for the longer Thames excursion routes, three rival operating companies vied to secure the business. These were the Victoria Steam Boat Association, the London, Woolwich & Clacton-on-Sea Steamboat Co, renowned for its fleet of smart 'Belle' steamers, and the General Steam Navigation Co, a concern which had

The famous *Lorna Doone* prior to having her promenade deck extended, passing the P&O liner *India*. *P&O*

One of the London & South Western Railway's steamers employed on the Portsmouth–Ryde ferry service, the *Duchess of Fife*, built in 1899.
Ian Allan Library

Campbell's *Brighton Queen*, the most famous of the cross-Channel excursion ships in the years before World War 1.
R. C. Riley collection

these waters up until the late 1950s, when its steamer services were finally withdrawn altogether.

General Steam Navigation's fleet included the *Eagle* of 1898, perpetuating a famous name first bestowed upon the company's original steamer built in 1820 at Brockelbank's yard at Deptford and later on an equally epic vessel, the second of the name, constructed at Northfleet, Kent, in 1853. The latter *Eagle*, a 325-gross-ton vessel, was in her day the fastest excursion steamer on the Thanet run.

To complete this preliminary circuit of the British coastline, some mention should be made of the comparatively minor paddle-ferry services that were operated across the mouth of the River Humber between Hull in Yorkshire and New Holland in Lincolnshire, and, further north, across the Firth of Forth. In both cases, the construction of road bridges at a later date eliminated the demand for ferry crossings, but in the early years of the 20th century they remained the only means of avoiding a long and circuitous journey. Both operations were railway-owned, on the Humber by the North Eastern Railway while the Forth services were run by the North British Railway. The North Eastern Railway's fleet of four vessels comprised the *Grimsby* (1888) and the *Cleethorpes* (1903) along with two new steamers, the *Brocklesby* and the *Killingholme*, both introduced in 1912.

The outbreak of World War 1 in September 1914 was to bring far-reaching social changes to Great Britain, no less to the paddle-steamer excursion trade, which would truly blossom

Belle of the East Coast, the *Southwold Belle*, one of three large steamers operated by London & Clacton Steam Packet Co, which entered service in 1900.
R. C. Riley collection

The *Mercury* again, a coloured postcard showing her with pale grey hull.
R. C. Riley collection

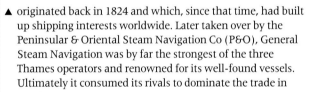

▲ originated back in 1824 and which, since that time, had built up shipping interests worldwide. Later taken over by the Peninsular & Oriental Steam Navigation Co (P&O), General Steam Navigation was by far the strongest of the three Thames operators and renowned for its well-found vessels. Ultimately it consumed its rivals to dominate the trade in

Each summer David MacBrayne ran tours on the Highland Royal Route with the 1878-built *Columba*, shown here, and the even older *Iona*, introduced 14 years earlier. They were among the oldest excursion paddle steamers still in operation at the time of their retirement in 1936. *R. C. Riley Collection*

The *Yarmouth Belle* in a postcard published by Belle Steamers before World War 1. Hand-coloured pictures like these also featured on the covers of the company's brochures. For a time, the Belle Steamers ships had an unusual V-shaped patch painted in red outlined with white on either side of the hull at the bows. *David L. Williams Collection*

One of the most popular of the excursion steamers that worked the London–Margate service along the Thames, the General Steam Navigation's *Eagle* of 1898. *R. C. Riley collection*

in the years between the end of this conflict and the start of the next. Meanwhile, for the duration, all pleasure cruises were suspended, and many regular ferry services were also curtailed as a large part of the paddle-steamer fleet was diverted to war work. Among them, a group of 70 steamers, including the entire Thames excursion fleet, saw service with the Royal Navy as minesweepers, undertaking duties in the English Channel, the North Sea and the Clyde Estuary. One squadron was transferred to the Mediterranean, arriving in convoy at Malta in July 1916. They were employed sweeping

Among the paddle steamers taken over by the Admiralty for service in the Mediterranean were four Red Funnel vessels — the *Princess Mary*, *Queen*, *Stirling Castle* and *Duchess of York*. Two were lost during this tour of duty, the *Stirling Castle* barely two months after her arrival; she struck a mine off the west coast of Malta on 26 September 1916. The *Princess Mary* was sunk after the war's end when, on 2 August 1919, prior to her return to the United Kingdom, she had the misfortune to run onto the wreck of the battleship HMS *Majestic*, which had fallen victim to an enemy submarine on 26 May 1915, during the early operations in the Dardanelles. The bottom was torn out of the *Princess Mary* and she was declared a total loss.

Another Red Funnel ship, the *Bournemouth Queen*, commissioned as HMS *Bourne*, had a lucky escape. While sweeping a large minefield in the Moray Firth, a mine exploded under her bow, shaking her from stem to stern and showering her decks with fragments of the device.

Other paddle steamers, like Red Funnel's *Balmoral* and General Steam Navigation's new *Golden Eagle*, were employed as transports, ferrying units of the British Expeditionary Force to France. Chartered by the Transport Department of the Ministry of Defence in February 1915, the *Balmoral* made a single troop-carrying crossing to Le Havre with a full complement of 680 troops, after which she was converted for minesweeping. Transport work really suited the larger, long-distance paddle vessels such as the *Empress Queen*, although she became another war casualty while performing these very duties. On 3 February 1916, when returning to Southampton virtually empty, apart from a cargo of ammunition, she ran aground on the Ring Rocks off Bembridge, Isle of Wight. In recognition of the brave rescue of the stricken ferry's crew, the coxswain of the local lifeboat was awarded the RNLI Silver Medal.

It took a while for postwar ferry and excursion operations to return to anything like their prewar level, but in just a few years, as the market began to show signs of expansion, many of the remaining veteran craft were paid off, to be replaced by new, superior paddle vessels.

P. & A. Campbell's *Westward Ho* as converted for minesweeping duties in World War 1.
Maritime Photo Library

▲ mines laid in the approaches to Gallipoli, around forward-base islands in the Greek Archipelago and in the channel leading to the entrance of the Grand Harbour, Valletta.

In the course of their minesweeping duties, some of the gallant little paddle vessels were lost. P. & A. Campbell's *Brighton Queen*, built in 1897, was sunk off Nieuwport, on the Belgian coast just south of Ostend, on 6 October 1915, and its *Lady Ismay* was another casualty, near the Galloper lightship on 21 December 1915. A similar fate befell Caledonian Steam Packet Co's *Duchess of Hamilton*, which struck one of the mines she was trying to clear off Longsand on 29 November 1915. The crest from her paddle box was displayed for many years along with a number of others at Princes Street station, Edinburgh before its closure in 1965. (On this note, other crests of former paddle steamers can be found in Gourock railway station.)

▲ The Royal Navy minesweeper HMS *Atherstone*, later converted for commercial work on the River Medway.
Imperial War Museum — SP106

◄ Entering Grand Harbour, Valletta, HMS *Queen II* (ex-*Queen*) shows off her minesweeping gear, extending out above her counter stern.
Imperial War Museum — SP837

▲ P. & A. Campbell's *Ravenswood*, photographed at Bristol
on 20 September 1955. *R. C. Riley*

▲ Berthed in the harbour at Weymouth on 30 September 1962, the 66-year-old Cosens paddle pleasure steamer *Consul*. *R. C. Riley*

2. THE INTER-WAR YEARS

The Clyde Estuary and Loch Lomond

The reorganisation of the railways in 1923 reduced the number of concerns operating steamer services in the estuary and the upper reaches of the Clyde to just four. Already, in 1919, Williamson and Buchanan had combined their operations to form one of only two remaining non-railway fleet owners. The other, David MacBrayne's, was still operating a number of paddle steamers on its longer-distance 'Royal Route to the Highlands and Islands', as it was known.

From the great rail reorganisation two very large and powerful railway companies emerged, responsible for services in Scotland, one being the London, Midland & Scottish (LMS) Railway, which included the Caledonian Railway and the Glasgow & South Western Railway. The other was the London & North Eastern Railway (LNER), incorporating the old North British Railway. Arising from this, the railway steamer services became divided on north/south lines; Craigendoran, the only railway port on the north shore, was an LNER stronghold, whereas the LMS steamers operated from the railway piers along the Ayrshire coast, on the south side of the river, at Gourock, Wemyss Bay, Fairlie and Ardrossan. From these various points, fed by express trains from Glasgow, steamer services radiated out to the many piers on the lochs and islands along the Firth and further afield.

During the summer season, a service was operated along the River Clyde from the heart of Glasgow, departing from the Bridge Wharf terminus and affording the passengers excellent views of the ships under construction at the shipyards on Clydebank, at Paisley and Govan. However, as a rather long-winded passage, it tended to be confined to cruise passengers, regular travellers preferring to use the combined rail and ferry services for quicker journey times.

Over the course of a typical year, between four and five million passengers were conveyed by the Clyde steamer fleet, many as excursionists in the summer months. In those days a trip 'doon the watter' was a particularly appealing outing for

the citizens of the great city of Glasgow; it was a form of escape from the drudgery of city life that was regularly taken, and for the steamer companies provided a welcome swelling of passenger numbers. Favourite destinations were Dunoon in Argyllshire, out to Rothesay on the Isle of Bute and through the Kyles of Bute, calling at Tighnabruaich, and on to Inverary.

Pleasure cruises were also available on Loch Lomond, the operator at that time being still, to some extent, independent of the railway companies. Later, LMS and LNER ran the service as a joint venture, taking over the two existing vessels *Prince Edward* and *Princess May*. For those who wanted and could afford it, a round trip could be made from Inverary, taking a bus link to Tarbet and then, from the southern end of Loch Lomond, connecting with the train from Balloch back to Glasgow — a full day's outing.

These were years of expansion for steamer ferry services and pleasure cruises everywhere, not least on the Clyde. The irregular sailings with, at times, badly maintained, inferior tonnage, that had characterised the Victorian age, were a thing of the past. Competition between the various operators acted as a powerful stimulus for fleet improvement and for enhanced quality of service. Hence the rival companies brought out some of their most splendid, most comfortably appointed vessels in the brief 20-year interlude to 1939. Indeed, there had been no new paddle steamers introduced on the Clyde routes since 1903, but, over a period of just six years from 1931, no fewer than seven new paddlers entered service, supplementing the best of the older craft that had been retained.

The LNER was the catalyst of the building programme when it brought out the stylish *Jeanie Deans* in 1931. Not only was the famine of new construction broken with the introduction of the *Jeanie Deans* but she also launched an era of large, powerful paddlers targeted at the long-distance excursion trade as an alternative to the turbine steamers, operating from points where water depth was limited.

The *Jeanie Deans* was the product of the Fairfield shipyard. She measured 635 gross tons when completed, with dimensions

◀◀ The *Jeanie Deans*, painted in Caledonian Steam Packet colours after the nationalisation of British Railways in 1948, makes a departure from Rothesay. *Ian Allan Library*

◀◀ A stern view of the *Jeanie Deans* underway on the Clyde. *Ian Allan Library*

The LMS's *Caledonia*, with her sister *Mercury*, introduced the so-called 'streamlined' or concealed paddle box. They were also among the first paddle steamers to adopt cruiser sterns in place of the old-fashioned counter. Viewed broadside-on, they could easily be mistaken for turbine steamers. This view of the *Caledonia* was taken in July 1951. *Ian Allan Library*

NEW SUPER TURBINE

King George V.

To CAMPBELTOWN, INVERARAY ETC.

QUEEN ALEXANDRA

KING EDWARD

MACHRIHANISH TOUR

FAMED LOCH ECK TOUR

IN CONNECTION WITH L.M.S & L.N.E.R. RAILWAYS.

JOHN WILLIAMSON & Cº 99 Great Clyde St., GLASGOW.

of 251ft (76.4m) overall length and 30ft (9.2m) across her paddle boxes. Her triple-expansion, three-crank engines — the first machinery of the type to be fitted to a Clyde steamer — gave her a speed of 18.5 knots. Although she was beautifully proportioned, her original, rather squat funnels spoiled her appearance; they were later lengthened, unevenly at first, but in their final configuration they enhanced her good looks. Later, the addition of enclosed observation lounges to her upper deck gave her a revised gross tonnage of 814.

In her fifth season, the *Jeanie Deans* performed a most unusual duty, providing an excursion platform for a vast complement, yet without moving an inch. It was March 1936, and the new Cunarder *Queen Mary* was heading down the Clyde to commence sea trials. It was the closed season for the pleasure steamers, but thousands of sightseers were expected for the great occasion. With the *Jeanie Deans* laid up in her winter quarters at Bowling

Harbour, the LNER saw an opportunity to satisfy a lot of customers while making some extra revenue. Thus she was opened up for the day as a static, floating grandstand. The *Jeanie Deans'* normal employment was on the excursion run to the Ayrshire coast and to the Isle of Arran, but she undertook regular service sailings too, from Craigendoran to Lochgoilhead and Arrochar.

In 1934 the LMS (Caledonian Steam Packet) responded with the sisters *Caledonia* and *Mercury*, commemorating earlier vessels of the same name. In this pair a great tradition was broken, for they did not have ornate paddle boxes with their decorative scrollwork, a feature which had been a source of pride in the long tradition of Clyde paddlers. Instead, they had a streamlined structure built over the paddle wheels, extending the enclosed passenger accommodation out to their full beam. While this afforded a sheltered viewpoint from which the open engine spaces could be conveniently inspected to great advantage, it was a modification that did not go down well with the traditionalists. Built respectively by Denny Bros at Dumbarton and Fairfield's yard in Glasgow, the 624-gross-ton *Caledonia* and *Mercury* had triple-expansion diagonal machinery with which they could achieve a speed of just over 17 knots. Their overall length was 224ft (68.2m) and extreme beam was 30ft (9.2m).

The first threat to paddle steamers had been in the form of the express turbine steamer, beginning in 1901 with the *King Edward*, the first commercial vessel to be powered by turbines. This colourful poster heralded the entry into service of the *King George V* in May 1928. Though fast, the turbine steamers were less manœuvrable and were compelled to avoid shallow-water piers.

The single-funnelled *Talisman*, introduced by LNER in 1935, was completed by A. & J. Inglis. She was 215ft (65.5m) in length and 28ft (8.4m) across the beam, with a gross tonnage of 544. Whereas paddle boxes of a conventional design were retained, she had a claim to fame for another radical feature. This was her novel (for a paddle vessel) and innovative main machinery, for she was a diesel-electric-powered vessel (DEPV). Essentially she had the same type of engines as those currently installed on the Cunard liner *Queen Elizabeth 2*. The *Talisman*'s engine installation comprised four vertical four-stroke diesel engines coupled to direct-current generators.

The electric current was fed to a double-armature motor mounted on the paddle shaft. She was the first paddle vessel in the world to have engines of this type. It proved to be a very economical power system: the *Talisman* could run for 100 miles on 1.5 tons of fuel oil, compared with older coal-burning paddlers which would have required 11.5 tons of coal to cover the same distance.

Just a year later, LMS introduced the small *Marchioness of Lorne* to run all-year-round regular services between Gourock and the residential piers at Kilcreggan, Blairmore, Kirn and Dunoon, carrying commuter traffic to and from the express

trains heading in and out of Glasgow. Designed to handle the Clyde crossing in fair weather and foul, she was built for comfort rather than speed. Her triple-expansion diagonal engines — by then the standard configuration for Clyde steamers — gave her the modest service speed of just 12 knots. The *Marchioness of Lorne* was also built by Fairfield. At only 427 gross tons she was the smallest of the new paddlers which entered the Clyde services in this period. Her principal dimensions were 200ft (60.8m) length and 27ft (8.3m) extreme beam.

The rivalry between the LMS and LNER on the River Clyde during the 1930s was comparable to that on their respective rail routes north to Scotland from London. Just as the great Pacific locomotives hauling the 'Coronation Scot' and 'Silver Jubilee' trains vied for speed honours on the West and East Coast main lines, so it was with the paddle pleasure steamers darting back and forth across the Clyde's broad expanse. By comparison, the races between the paddle steamers were sedate affairs, thrilling for the passengers but at a relaxed pace all the same.

In 1937 the LMS added its boldest challengers to date, the large paddlers *Juno* and *Jupiter*. This striking duo recalled the vessels of the old Glasgow & South Western Railway, which had always been named after planets and stars. Like the *Caledonia*, *Mercury* and *Marchioness of Lorne*, the

Looking like a smaller version ▲ of the *Caledonia* and *Mercury*, the *Marchioness of Lorne* was built for the all-year-round residential service linking Gourock with Kilcreggan, Dunoon and the other commuter piers at the southern end of Loch Long.
Ian Allan Library

The *Jupiter* approaching ▶ Gourock pier. She was laid down on 29 October 1936 and launched the following spring, on 9 April 1937.
Ian Allan Library

twin-funnelled *Juno* and *Jupiter* had enclosed or streamlined paddle boxes. At 642 gross tons, these vessels were 231ft (70.3m) in overall length and 30ft (9.2m) across their beam, slightly larger but somewhat shorter than LNER's *Jeanie Deans*. In keeping with the machinery fashion of the time, the *Juno* and *Jupiter* also had triple-expansion diagonal engines giving them a service speed of 17.5 knots. Spark-arresters were fitted in their funnels to prevent furnace cinders from falling on passengers on the open decks.

Besides these new vessels, many prewar paddlers were still running on the Clyde — the *Lucy Ashton*, *Marmion* and *Waverley* for the LNER and the *Duchess of Fife*, *Duchess of Rothesay*, *Marchioness of Breadalbane* and *Glen Rosa* for the LMS. Williamson-Buchanan had five vessels in operation, including the *Isle of Arran*, *Kylemore* and *Queen Empress*, all of which passed into Caledonian Steam Packet (LMS) ownership in 1935. Williamson-Buchanan's days were effectively numbered from that time, although the company remained in existence for another eight years.

David MacBrayne's luxurious paddle ships employed on the Oban run could still be seen on the Clyde until 1936. In that year the 58-year-old *Columba* and the 72-year-old *Iona* finally gave way to turbine vessels when the ships of Turbine Steamers Ltd passed, respectively, into LMS and MacBrayne ownership.

◄ A blinding snowstorm caught out the *Lucy Ashton* while crossing the Clyde to Craigendoran one winter. In the white-out conditions she ran into an Atlantic liner moored in the Gareloch, awaiting her passengers, causing quite a shock to all concerned besides a measure of damage. In May 1948, when she celebrated her diamond jubilee, the *Lucy Ashton* attained a greater age than any other railway steamer so far built. *Ian Allan Library*

◄ London & North Eastern Railway's *Marmion*, built in 1906, was a casualty of World War 2, being bombed and sunk by enemy aircraft in April 1941. She had a similar overall appearance to the *Lucy Ashton*, but, unlike her North British fleet-mate, the *Marmion*'s bridge extended across her full width and she lacked the high saloon structure abaft the funnel. *Ian Allan Library*

The London, Midland & Scottish Railway steamer *Caledonia* — a post-World War 2 view in British Railways (Caledonian Steam Packet) colours, revealing the absence of conventional paddle boxes. She was converted for oil-burning in 1945.
World Ship Society – 3851

The diesel-electric paddle vessel *Talisman* at Wemyss Bay on 12 June 1956.
John Edgington

With so much traffic on the river, much of it vying for the same business, the manœuvring around the pier heads had once been a frantic affair, with competing vessels trying to get alongside ahead of their rivals. This potentially dangerous process of racing for the vacant berth in order to collect the lion's share of the waiting passengers had been brought to an end back in the late 1800s by the introduction of a unique signalling system which continued in use between the wars. Devised by Charles Allan, a leading light of the Allan Line shipping family, it was erected on every pier along the length of the Clyde.

The system comprised a large, triangular structure mounted above the pier-head building, arranged in such a way that two of its faces were directed towards the river at the approaching steamers. In the window on each face were three prominent discs laid out in a horizontal row, their colours being black for danger (stand off) or white for clear (safe to approach).

At the piermaster's discretion, the signals would be changed to advise which steamer could come alongside, an interlocking system preventing a signal from being changed (from black to white) if a berth was already occupied. If the right disc of the three were changed to white, the furthest to starboard of the approaching steamers on that side of the pier could come alongside. Similarly, the central and left signals acted as the authority to proceed, respectively, for the vessels at the centre or on the extreme portside of the group waiting off the pier. Those steamers not invited forward were required to lay off at a safe distance until they received the appropriate signal. The system was also used to control movements when steamers approached from different directions.

The value of the signalling system can be readily appreciated, for some of the busiest piers, such as Dunoon and Rothesay, could have as many as 40 arrivals per day and an equal number of departures during times of intense activity.

▲ Built alongside her sister, the war casualty *Juno*, the London, Midland & Scottish Railway's *Jupiter* shown leaving Wemyss Bay in June 1956. The *Juno* and *Jupiter* were designed for all-year-round scheduled service work rather than summer excursions alone, a distinction that was reflected in their heavier scantlings. The *Jupiter* took the name of an earlier 1896-built paddler which was broken up at Barrow from December 1935. *John Edgington*

The Bristol Channel and Southwest England

Following the end of World War 1 and the return of its vessels from Admiralty service, P. & A. Campbell set about reinforcing its dominant position on the Bristol Channel through a programme of renovation and renewal. At the beginning of the 1920s, its West Country fleet comprised eight vessels:

Barry (1907)	477grt	Glen Avon (1912)	509grt
Britannia (1896)	459grt	Glen Usk (1914)	524grt
Cambria (1895)	438grt	Ravenswood (1891)	391grt
Devonia (1905)	520grt	Westward Ho (1894)	438grt

(P. & A. Campbell's South Coast operations based at Brighton, which were not resumed until 1923, are covered in the next section.)

The Campbells had introduced their latest excursion vessel, the *Glen Usk*, just prior to World War 1. Completed by the Ailsa Shipbuilding Co at Troon, Ayrshire, she was an elegant single-funnelled vessel, with a length of 232ft (70.7m) and a beam of 28ft (8.5m); diagonal compound engines gave her a maximum speed of 17 knots and a service speed of 14 knots.

In October 1919 the company went back to the Ailsa shipyard for an enlarged and improved steamer of the same type, the *Glen Gower*. Launched on 14 February 1922 by the wife of Captain Alec Campbell, she entered service on the Swansea–Ilfracombe route on 3 June 1922. The twin-funnelled *Glen Gower* measured 553 tons gross on dimensions of 242ft (73.9m) length overall and 28.5ft (8.7m) beam. Service speed with a near-identical engine arrangement was comparable to that of the *Glen Usk*.

For P. & A. Campbell the return to commercial operations after World War 1 saw a resurgence of competition on the company's established route network. The rival, Cardiff-based 'Yellow Funnel' fleet of W. H. Tucker was pursuing the trade that the Campbells had, in the prewar years, almost taken for granted as being theirs. In fact, Tucker had just two ships, the *Lady Evelyn* and the *Lady Moyra*, formerly the *Gwalia* and a sister vessel to the Campbells' *Devonia*; ironically, the competing pair frequently arrived simultaneously off the same resorts while running identical excursions.

Tucker's threat did not endure for long. By 1923, P. & A. Campbell had acquired the Cardiff company and its assets, absorbing the *Lady Moyra* into the Bristol Channel operations and re-launching its South Coast services with the *Lady Evelyn*, suitably renamed *Brighton Belle*. The reintroduction of the Brighton-based operation necessitated the transfer of other vessels in order to maintain a full excursion programme there. Thus from 1923 the *Devonia* and *Ravenswood* were also removed from the West Country roster and relocated in Sussex.

The remaining eight saloon steamers supported a wide variety of excursion routes, some of longer duration to Minehead and Weston-super-Mare or to Ilfracombe and Lundy Island, others of half-day length or evening cruises encompassing Cardiff and Penarth, Barry Island, Clevedon, Swansea and Porthcawl. One cruise took passengers out to and around the Scarweather lightship, but it is hard to imagine the appeal that such a maritime feature had to offer. Visits to Lundy Island and certain other destinations were interesting, to say the least, for the paddle steamers had to anchor offshore while local boatmen ferried the passengers to and from the beaches. This was all very well on warm, calm days but it could be a risky and unpleasant business — for the passengers — in cold, windy or wet conditions.

For generations, mariners on the Bristol Channel have used the visibility of Lundy Island as a convenient measure of the imminent weather:

> Lundy high, it will be dry;
> Lundy low, it will be snow;
> Lundy plain, it will be rain;
> Lundy in haze, fine for days

… so the rhyme goes. It is an interesting and revealing fact, duly recorded in the ships' logs and other operational records maintained by the P. & A. Campbell company, that long spells of inclement weather were as much a phenomenon of the summers of the early 1920s as they have been in more recent years. In those days, of course, they did not put such unseasonable conditions down to 'global warming'.

Occasionally weather and tide conspired to make real difficulties for the little paddlers, such as on 12 July 1926, when the speedy *Cambria* ran aground at Rilledge Point (near Ilfracombe) in fog, leaving her forward end high and dry.

◀◀ The *Britannia*, with the *Cambria* and *Westward Ho*, remained popular excursion vessels until September 1939 when another World War interrupted these services for the next six years. All three were re-boilered and extensively refurbished in the early 1920s.
Ian Allan Library

◀◀ Along with her sisters *Glen Usk* and *Lady Ismay*, the *Glen Avon* was one of Campbell's newest ships prior to the outbreak of World War 1. Of the three vessels, the *Lady Ismay* did not survive the war at sea.
Ian Allan Library

▲ Another Campbell steamer photographed at Bristol on
20 September 1955, the *Britannia*, one of three new vessels
introduced by P. & A. Campbell from 1894 as the company rapidly
enhanced the size and quality of its Bristol Channel fleet.
R. C. Riley

▲ A view of the small wooden River Dart paddler *Kingswear Castle* taken at Chatham while she was running Medway cruises following her rescue and renovation by the Paddle Steamer Preservation Society. *David Reed — 00957*

cruises concentrated on the South Devon coastal resorts, taking in Teignmouth, Dawlish and Exmouth. Connecting cruises permitted trips into Dartmouth Harbour, past Brixham, or along the River Tamar. Despite the evident attraction of excursions along this enticingly picturesque stretch of coastline, the lack of suitable piers meant that they were mainly only sightseeing tours with limited opportunities for visits ashore. The experiment did not last long, no doubt curtailed because the prospect of long hours restricted to the steamer's decks held less appeal.

Another company, the River Dart Steamboat Co, exploited the inland delights of the River Dart, in South Devon, with a series of small wooden-hulled paddlers whose dimensions were confined to the limits imposed by the navigable channels. These smart little vessels were totally unique, unlike anything operated elsewhere in British coastal waters and exhibiting a distinctive profile. They had a low freeboard, permitted by the sheltered waters in which they operated, a single funnel set immediately abaft the small, enclosed bridge and open decks arranged around a small central saloon, providing modest refreshments. The hull ended in a convex curved stem with decorative scrollwork on either side of the bows. The rear sun-deck was split into two levels with fixed stanchions in the lower section permitting it to be covered by canvas awnings in hot or wet weather.

Two vessels of this type, measuring approximately 95 gross tons, were introduced in the 1920s — the *Totnes Castle* in 1923 and the *Kingswear Castle* in 1924. The pair joined the very similar *Compton Castle*, which had been introduced in 1914, and the 1907-built *Dartmouth Castle*, making a fleet of four excursion steamers.

Local boatmen ferry passengers to the shore on Lundy Island from the new *Glen Gower*, in a scene captured on camera between the wars.
Maritime Photo Library

▲ The *Cambria* was carrying some 400 or so passengers at the time, a fair number of whom made it ashore across the rocks after clambering down from her bows. Others were ferried into Ilfracombe in the *Cambria*'s lifeboats. The steamer herself floated off at the next high tide with barely a scratch — a testament to her solid construction, over 30 years earlier, by McIntyre's.

The Campbells' West Country services were primarily focused on the Bristol Channel, linking the North Devon and Somerset coastal resorts with South Wales and the rivers Severn and Avon. In 1932 and again in 1933 the company embarked upon a new venture on the South Devon coastline using the *Westward Ho*, one of its older and smaller vessels. Centred on Plymouth and Torquay, cruises were offered to places as far afield as Weymouth and Bournemouth and, in a westerly direction, to Looe and Penzance. Other, shorter

▲ Forging her way along the River Dart with a full complement of passengers, the River Dart paddle steamer, the *Compton Castle*. *Maritime Photo Library*

◀ This view looking down on the *Totnes Castle* shows off particularly well the open foredeck of these distinctive, small wooden paddlers, operated exclusively on the River Dart in South Devon. The decorative scrollwork at the bow was a feature of the *Totnes Castle* and her consorts. *Maritime Photo Library*

The stylish *Balmoral* running at speed. Though she was an essential unit of the Southampton & Isle of Wight Steam Packet fleet, in order to combat aggressive competition, she was nevertheless costly to run and something of a mixed blessing to her owners.
Red Funnel Group

A late-1930s view of the *Lorna Doone* rounding the Needles rocks, at the Isle of Wight's extreme western tip, during a round-the-island sightseeing cruise.
Red Funnel Group

The South Coast

The famous quartered house flag of the Southampton, Isle of Wight & South Coast Royal Mail Steam Packet (Red Funnel), proudly flown from its fleet of ships, was a potent symbol of the company's dominance of the Isle of Wight central passage and Solent excursion services between the wars. Well known for the mnemonic rhyme 'Blue to mast, green to fly; red on deck, white on high', it was derived from the four early steamers *Sapphire, Emerald, Ruby* and *Pearl*. Just as the Clyde steamers exuded a certain distinct Scottish flavour, so the Red Funnel vessels were synonymous with the southern coastal scene, their rails crowded in the season with smiling holidaymakers enjoying the bracing sea breezes.

World War 1 had cost the company the new paddler *Princess Mary* and the older *Stirling Castle*, but it nevertheless retained a large fleet that was a *tour de force* when ranked against its rivals in the region. At the resumption of peacetime services, no fewer than 11 steamers were engaged on regular packet services to and from the Isle of Wight, including the 1876-built *Lord Elgin*, which had been converted for an exclusive cargo-carrying role in 1910, or on seasonal excursions of long or short duration.

Best known as Red Funnel Steamers, the company did not generally adopt the colours from which it ultimately took its name until 1935. Before that, the funnels had been either all white or white with a black top. Red funnels with black tops had been introduced first on the Bournemouth-based steamers serving Swanage between 1910 and 1914.

With the exception of a small number of paddlers which were out-and-out excursion craft, and the already mentioned *Lord Elgin*, all Red Funnel ships were required to undertake a mix of three essential duties — regular passage work between Southampton and the Isle of Wight, short cruises in the peak season and tendering service to the great ocean liners which made the Solent their UK terminus. It is unlikely that, but for the lively encroachment on their patch of P. & A. Campbell's *Cambria* around the turn of the century, Red Funnel would have deviated from this policy and committed to investment in the three pure excursion ships *Balmoral, Lorna Doone* and *Bournemouth Queen*. In the event, with the threat soon withdrawn, the *Balmoral*, in particular, was left something of a costly burden on the company, spending more time idle than engaged in revenue-earning service.

The other units of the fleet at the beginning of the 1920s included the three similar, Barclay Curle-built ships *Princess Beatrice* (1880), *Princess Helena* (1883) and *Her Majesty* (1885). There was also the *Solent Queen* (1889), which had been built as a replacement for another new paddler, the *Princess of Wales*, lost in a collision during her builder's trials in June 1888, the similar *Prince of Wales* (1891) and the *Duchess of York* (1896). The last was renamed *Duchess of Cornwall* in 1928 when Canadian Pacific requested her former name for one of its quartet of new St Lawrence-service express-mail liners. Last but not least was the *Queen* (1902), which also underwent an interesting change of name. In an arrangement with Cunard

▲ On 12 September 1931 the *Bournemouth Queen* made a special excursion from Bournemouth to view the flying display by the British Schneider Trophy team, which had secured the trophy outright when, in the absence of any contest, they clocked up three straight wins.

◀ A prewar view of the *Bournemouth Queen*, another of Red Funnel's dedicated cruise vessels, as built with a white-painted funnel. *Red Funnel Group*

Line, she was registered as the *Mauretania* for two years from 1936 in order to preserve the illustrious name so that it could be bestowed upon a new intermediate liner, launched at Birkenhead on 28 July 1938. Thereafter, the former *Queen* was renamed *Corfe Castle*, a name she retained until the end of her career, a year later.

Red Funnel's excursion routes were concentrated not only on Southampton, as might be expected, but also on Bournemouth, arising from the acquisition of the Bournemouth & South Coast Steam Packets back in 1908. Smaller, less powerful vessels worked the shorter routes from Bournemouth to Swanage, Weymouth and the Isle of Wight and from Southampton to Ryde and Southsea, as well as around the Island. The longer cruises to Torquay and Dartmouth, to Brighton and Eastbourne and, via Sandown and Shanklin, across the Channel to Cherbourg were maintained by the larger and faster 1900-built *Balmoral*.

From the earliest times, besides passengers and mails, many Red Funnel vessels carried a quantity of cars on the regular sailings of the Southampton–Cowes service. It was a hint of the transition in coastal ferry services that was to occur barely a quarter of a century later. The paddlers with this capability could be readily distinguished by their ideally suited open well-deck forward. This design had been introduced with the *Southampton* built in 1872, its original purpose having been lower-class passenger space — a rather inhospitable area exposed to inclement weather, especially on vessels which did not have a raised forecastle. On some ships the foremast, stepped from this forward deck, was either repositioned or removed completely to leave an unobstructed stowage area, providing more vehicle space and allowing easier handling.

A fleet-replacement and renewal programme was initiated by Red Funnel in 1927 with the *Princess Elizabeth*, a vessel which, in many respects, was closely similar to the *Princess Mary* which had sunk in the Mediterranean nine years earlier. Built in Southampton by Day, Summers & Co, she measured 388 gross tons and had dimensions of 195ft (59.5m) length and 24ft (7.4m) beam. She was fitted with coal-fired, compound diagonal steam engines giving her a best speed of 14.5 knots. Unlike earlier Red Funnel vessels of this general configuration, she lacked the enclosed alleyways on the lower deck aft, her

first-class saloon extending the full width of the ship. The lounge, on the deck beneath, also occupied her full beam. A main mast was added later.

As an indication that change was in the air, Red Funnel's next new building, the *Medina*, was a propeller-driven motor vessel. She was of similar size and proportions to the smaller paddle steamers, but her modern profile heralded a look that was to be perpetuated, albeit with improvements, in the later and larger twin-screw *Vecta* (1938) and *Balmoral* (1949).

The emergence of the *Medina* did not signify the end of Red Funnel's paddle-steamer era — far from it. Indeed, its very next new ferry was a paddler — the smart little *Gracie Fields*, which entered service in 1936, named after the most popular singer and film star in the land. She was launched by her patron at Thornycroft's Woolston yard, to the strains of her popular hit-song 'Sing As We Go', thrilling the watching crowds. The *Gracie Fields* was virtually the same size as the earlier *Princess Elizabeth* and of near-identical appearance too. She could be distinguished from her older fleet-mate by her raised forecastle, which she had from the outset, and a deck strake that extended across her paddle boxes. Below the waterline she was fitted with a bow rudder, another enhancement which differentiated her from the *Princess Elizabeth*.

The *Gracie Fields*, along with the *Princess Elizabeth*, *Duchess of Cornwall*, *Her Majesty* and, when she was not otherwise engaged on excursion work, the *Lorna Doone*, was frequently used to tender such great liners as French Line's *Normandie* and Norddeutscher Lloyd's *Bremen* and *Europa* when they anchored off Cowes or Ryde. The keen observer could always tell when the paddlers were employed on these duties, for they carried special cages, stowed on deck, which were used to hoist or lower passengers' luggage and mail packages from the lofty decks of the liners.

During her third season, while bound for Cowes on the packet service in July 1939, the *Gracie Fields* was involved in an unusual accident. While passing the Royal Naval Air Station at Calshot Spit, as she entered the Solent packed with holidaymakers, a young aviator attempted a stunt take-off across her bow. The daring or reckless manœuvre, depending on one's point of view, ended in disaster. Misjudging the distance and elevation on the take-off run, the aircraft failed

◄◄ The *Gracie Fields* beneath the stern of the great French Line passenger liner *Normandie* while tendering her in the Solent. *Red Funnel Group*

The grandeur of the passenger accommodation at the height of the paddle steamer's glory days is evident in these scenes taken aboard Red Funnel vessels during the 1930s — the dining room aboard the *Gracie Fields*, with tablecloths, napkins and vases of fresh flowers (*right*); Lloyd Loom chairs and upholstered seats in one of the *Balmoral*'s elegant passenger saloons (*below*); and the *Gracie Fields'* aft saloon, complete with mock fireplace (*bottom*). Heating in cold weather was actually provided by the sturdy radiator. *Red Funnel Group*

to clear the paddler. Its starboard wing struck the *Gracie Fields'* port bow and shattered, sustaining fatal damage. Careering over the deck, the unfortunate machine plunged into the sea, giving the pilot an unexpected early bath. The *Gracie Fields'* mast was felled in the accident, but luckily no one was seriously hurt and the damage to the Red Funnel ship turned out to be relatively minor — a miracle, when one considers what might otherwise have resulted.

Very occasionally, paddle steamers from all regions suffered embarrassing mechanical breakdown, but it seems that it was more commonly tide, weather, or flotsam and jetsam that brought grief upon them if they were to suffer a mishap. The *Duchess of Cornwall* was making the last crossing to Cowes on 18 April 1935 when she struck a submerged object as she passed Calshot Castle, seriously damaging one of her paddles. This was before the days when these vessels routinely carried ship-to-shore radio, and her unexplained failure to arrive at Cowes was soon causing concern. Eventually discovered in the early hours of the morning, she had to be towed back to Southampton. There her passengers transhipped to the *Medina*. Completely exhausted, they finally arrived on the Island at 7.00am on 19 April, having experienced possibly the longest ever crossing of the Solent!

Weather problems could be a real nuisance. In August 1932, the *Lorna Doone* and *Balmoral* were unable to proceed from Sandown Pier because of an unseasonable blanket of pea-soup-thick fog. Without radar and other modern aids to navigation, they were compelled to wait it out. Their combined complement of some 800 passengers were obliged to avail themselves of the temporary accommodation offered by the pier's Casino Theatre, while the services of the BBC were called upon to broadcast a message advising relatives of the delay. It was reminiscent of a similar hold-up in 1908, also in August, when the *Balmoral* was prevented from making the return crossing of a Cherbourg excursion because of thick fog in the Channel.

The introduction of the *Princess Elizabeth* and *Gracie Fields* and, of course, the *Medina* and later *Vecta* led to the disposal of a number of the older members of the Red Funnel fleet. The *Princess Beatrice* was retired in 1933, the *Prince of Wales* in 1938 and the *Corfe Castle* in 1939. All three were scrapped.

Along the coast a short distance at Portsmouth, the Southern Railway, one of the four creations of the great railway reorganisation, had its main terminus for the Isle of Wight services. In fact, the Southern Railway worked two Isle of Wight ferry routes, either side of Red Funnel — from Lymington to Yarmouth in the west and from Portsmouth to Ryde in the east. The Southern Railway had inherited a number of vessels from one of its predecessors, the London & South Western Railway, some now rather long in the tooth. The Southern Railway embarked upon an aggressive new-building programme, commissioning seven modern paddlers in the inter-war period: *Shanklin* (1924), *Freshwater* (1927),

▲ Southern Railway excursions by the trio of 'Duchesses' to view the warships assembled for the Royal Naval Review at Spithead on 26 July 1924.

◄ The first new paddle vessel built for the Southern Railway for its Isle of Wight services from Portsmouth was the *Shanklin*, which entered service in 1924. *Ian Allan Library*

Portsdown (1928), *Southsea* (1930), *Whippingham* (1930), *Sandown* (1934) and *Ryde* (1937). The *Southsea* and *Whippingham* measured 825 gross tons, were 254ft (77.4m) in length and could carry 1,200 passengers. The later pair, *Sandown* and *Ryde*, were slightly smaller at 684 gross tons and 223ft (68.0m) overall length but were the first paddle steamers to be fitted with three-cylinder engines rather than two-cylinder compound machinery. All four served the Portsmouth–Ryde ferry route, besides which the *Southsea* and *Whippingham* also made seasonal cruises.

Cosens of Weymouth was renowned for having in its fleet some of the oldest vessels on the British register. For instance, the 1846-built *Premier* was 92 years old when she made her last sailing, bound for the scrapyard. When Portland Harbour was thick with naval ships, the Cosens steamers were employed conveying the liberty men between ship and shore, the trip costing each sailor the equivalent of 4p. This function, along with cruising along the South Coast, were the mainstays of the business for the buff-funnelled Cosens ships. During the 1920s and 1930s the company had a fleet of eight vessels: *Consul*, *Embassy*, *Emperor of India*, *Empress*, *Majestic*, *Monarch*, *Premier* and *Victoria*. They either worked from Weymouth, making trips to Portland, Lulworth Cove, Lyme Regis and Torquay or sailings to Swanage, Bournemouth and the Isle of Wight, or were based at Poole or Bournemouth, working in the opposite

Ryde pierhead between the wars, with the *Shanklin* embarking passengers and loading mail and luggage. *Ian Allan Library*

The *Southsea* was the first of a second pair of new Southern Railway steamers which entered service in 1930. She was another war loss, in 1941. *Ian Allan Library*

Sister ship of the *Southsea*, the *Whippingham* held the distinction of rescuing the greatest number of soldiers in a single voyage during the evacuation of Dunkirk. The *Southsea* and *Whippingham* were the most stylish of the paddle steamers introduced by the Southern Railway, having a flush-decked design with rigid bulwarks forward. *Maritime Photo Library*

This picture, taken in the early days of British Railways, shows the former Southern Railway ships *Sandown* and *Ryde* tied up alongside each other in Portsmouth Harbour. They were the last paddle steamers built expressly for the Isle of Wight ferry services. Beyond them, to the left, is the funnel of one of the new postwar-built, screw-driven motor vessels of the 'Southsea' class. *Ian Allan Library*

direction to the Weymouth boats but also making excursions to Portsmouth Harbour and Southampton Docks.

The *Emperor of India* (ex-*Princess Royal*), built locally by John I. Thornycroft at Southampton, had been purchased in 1908 from Red Funnel, for which she had been ordered as new. The latter company had apparently rejected her because she did not perform to its requirements. The implication was that there were mechanical shortcomings, but the real reason for declining to accept her appears to have been connected with the distribution of her accommodation: it was very generous in its provision for First-class passengers but for Second-class, who could typically represent 75% of the passenger complement, there was only limited saloon space and minimal access to the open decks. On reflection, it was considered that her interior layout was better suited to single-class operation, whereas the Southampton–Cowes crossing called for two-class vessels. After operating her for no more than two or three weeks, Red Funnel returned her to the shipyard.

A pre-World War 1 vessel which later entered Cosens service, the *Embassy* arrives at Yarmouth, Isle of Wight, from Weymouth in August 1963. She was built in 1911 as the *Duchess of Norfolk* for the Isle of Wight ferry services. *Ray Sprake*

Painted in British Railways colours, the *Freshwater*, built originally for the Southern Railway, departs Lymington for Yarmouth, Isle of Wight on 18 July 1955. *R. C. Riley*

Though no longer a Red Funnel ship when this photograph was taken, the *Princess Elizabeth* retains the colours of her original owners. This view of her was taken in August 1963 during a cruise visit to the Isle of Wight. *Ray Sprake*

The 1934-built *Sandown*, a view of her taken on 28 September 1958 when she was a member of the British Railways Southern Region fleet. She is seen here berthed at Newhaven. *R. C. Riley*

The *Monarch* at the time of the 1929 Schneider Trophy competition, ferrying employees of the Supermarine aircraft works, in Southampton, to watch the races in the Solent. Note the Royal Navy's aircraft carrier *Furious* in the background.
Ian Allan Library

Cosens steamer *Empress* at Lulworth Cove on 17 July 1951. Boarding was across a precariously arranged gang-plank.
Ian Allan Library

In the event, Cosens did find the *Emperor of India* mechanically troublesome, her large paddle wheels causing the water to choke in her paddle boxes — a problem that could not, it seems, be cured. Nevertheless, she remained an active member of the fleet until the 1950s. Measuring 428 gross tons, she was 195ft 6in (59.6m) in length and 25ft (7.6m) across her beam. During World War 1 she served as a minesweeper under the name *Mahratta*.

Pride of the Cosens fleet, the elegant, twin-funnelled *Monarch*, built by R. & H. Green at Blackwall in 1888, remained a favourite. Typically steaming 14,000 miles in a season, she ran the company's banner excursions to such events as the Schneider Trophy races, the maiden voyages of the *Queen Mary* and other new passenger liners, and the Silver Jubilee (1935) and Coronation (1937) Fleet Reviews.

Following the acquisition of the Cardiff-based W. H. Tucker concern, P. & A. Campbell re-opened its South Coast operations in 1923 with the *Brighton Belle* (ex-*Lady Evelyn*). At the same time, the *Devonia* and *Ravenswood* were also switched to the excursion services based in Sussex. In consort, the three worked a programme of short coastal cruises to Eastbourne, Hastings and the Isle of Wight with occasional calls at Bognor Regis, Worthing and Newhaven. The Eastbourne trips took in Beachy Head and the Royal Sovereign lightship.

During the season, the steamers berthed overnight at Newhaven but, because the P. & A. Campbell overhaul and winter lay-up facilities were located at Bristol, between each season they had to transfer between the Sussex coast and the Bristol Channel — a far-from-ideal arrangement. The passage normally took around 28 hours to complete if the weather was kind, but tempestuous seas were often encountered in the English Channel and around the Lizard, and then it took a good deal longer.

A service to Boulogne and Calais, instituted before the war with the *Brighton Queen* (sunk in October 1915), was reinstated using the *Devonia*, *Brighton Belle* and *Ravenswood*. Of these, the latter pair were not sufficiently seaworthy for the open-water cross-Channel routes. Following a trip by the *Ravenswood*

The Campbell South Coast steamer *Brighton Belle*, formerly the Furness Railway steamer *Lady Evelyn*.
Maritime Photo Library

The *Devonia*, one of a pair of ships built as rivals to the Campbell steamers but which later joined the Campbell fleet. Her sister *Gwalia*, later renamed *Lady Moyra*, became the second *Brighton Queen* in May 1933.
R. C. Riley Collection

▲ along the coast to Folkestone in very bad weather in August 1923, which almost ended disastrously, she was returned to the Bristol Channel. Her place was filled from 1925 by the *Barry*, now renamed *Waverley*, pre-empting new certification rules introduced by the Board of Trade in 1926 which prohibited passenger vessels with open foredecks from making crossings to the Continent.

The imposition of yet more stringent regulations from 1933 similarly denied the appropriate certification to the *Waverley*, curtailing her cross-Channel career. She was replaced by the *Glen Gower*, although the *Waverley* remained on the South Coast making shorter, coastal excursions. On a positive note, the same year witnessed the return of a famous name to the Sussex itineraries when the former Furness Railway steamer *Lady Moyra* was transferred to this station, renamed *Brighton Queen*. It was an inspired move, elevating the popularity of P. & A. Campbell's day visits to Boulogne and Calais, and, occasionally, other French ports, for which the new *Brighton Queen* was soon renowned.

From 1937 the *Brighton Belle* reverted to the Bristol Channel services, leaving the former sisters *Devonia* and *Brighton Queen*, along with the *Waverley*, to maintain the South Coast operations for the few remaining years of peace.

The Thames, Medway and Humber services

The excursion routes on the Thames and its estuary, well established and populated with a sizeable fleet by the early 1920s, had developed from two distinct services. One was the so-called 'Long Ferry' from the Pool of London to Gravesend, calling at Greenwich and Woolwich; the other was the long-distance 'hoy' trade, named after the sailing hoys that had once plied the river, extending out to Margate and the other Thanet ports. The 'Long Ferry' service had been more-or-less eliminated when the railway line was extended to Gravesend in the mid-1800s. From that time the remaining passenger shipping activities on the river had concentrated on the pleasure-cruise trade over a route that extended for the length of the River Thames with various interim stops permitting long or short trips, as preferred. These cruises were particularly popular with the enormous numbers of holidaymakers by then being carried out to Margate and Ramsgate by the railways. The emergence of the Belle Steamers Co in 1890 opened up the coastal cruise business to the northern shore of the estuary, with services linking Southend-on-Sea with other resorts in Essex and further north on the East Anglian coast.

Just as the Thames services had comprised two original elements, so the vessels operated on them were largely products of two competing shipyards — Denny Bros of Dumbarton and the Fairfield shipyard on Clydeside. At first, a number of older Scottish saloon steamers had been brought south with great acclaim to run on the Thames, but in truth they were inferior to the standard then demanded by passengers on the Clyde routes. Recognising that the Thames services deserved quality vessels in their own right, the two Scottish builders saw an opportunity to exhibit their products to the marine industry in this conspicuous arena, even building some vessels as risk ventures and chartering them to the operators.

Things had settled down somewhat by the time of the period immediately after World War 1. The two remaining New Palace paddlers (following the transfer of the noteworthy *La Marguerite* to North Wales) had been reduced to just one — the *Royal Sovereign*, an 891-gross-ton-vessel built in 1893; having been laid up throughout the war, her earlier half-sister *Koh-i-noor* had been scrapped in 1918. These excursion steamers featured an upper promenade deck that continued for the full length of the hull. Designed to pass under London Bridge as far as the Old Swan Pier, their funnels could be lowered and their masts were hinged at the heel. They were capable of a maximum speed of almost 20 knots — a matter of concern along the shores of the river, for they generated a vigorous wash — and this permitted the round trip from the Pool to Margate and return to be completed in one day.

The *Royal Sovereign* served the General Steam Navigation Co on the Thanet run for one season, 1929, going to the breakers' yard in the Netherlands the following year. However, her name remained associated with the company and was given to a new cross-Channel motor vessel introduced in 1937 but lost at Dunkirk three years later.

In 1909 General Steam Navigation had introduced the *Golden Eagle* on the Thanet run, at 793 gross tons and nearly 300ft (91.5m) long almost as large as the *Royal Sovereign*. Built by the famous Clydebank yard of John Brown — birthplace of Cunard Line's 'Queens', the *Aquitania* and many other illustrious ships — she was distinguished by having her side plating taken up to the upper deck for the length of her fore end, right out to the stem. This made

The old *Royal Sovereign* ran in consort with the *London Belle* for the 1926 Holiday Season, sailing from North Woolwich Pier to Southend, Essex, and the Thanet resorts. After working for one year for General Steam Navigation, in 1929, the *Royal Sovereign* was sold for scrapping. For years the *Royal Sovereign* featured as one of the many vessels of the Penny Fleet Review, which marked the opening of the Thames cruise season.

A classic General Steam Navigation poster from the 1930s, promoting the Eagle Steamers One-Day cruises. The steamer is the *Royal Eagle*, launched on 24 February 1932 and introduced to the Thames services that summer. *P&O*

A wonderfully evocative painting by marine artist Alfred Leete of the *Crested Eagle* steaming through the Thames Estuary, returning to London in late August 1939 on her final commercial voyage. The sinking of the *Crested Eagle* at Dunkirk resulted in the single costliest loss of life of the entire operation. *Private Collection*

her a better sea-boat when rough weather was encountered, besides providing useful additional enclosed passenger accommodation. She was a fast vessel and soon earned a good reputation with passengers. Dubbed 'the happy ship', she was an enduring favourite.

The stylish and innovative *Crested Eagle* which came to be known as the 'Greyhound of the River' joined the *Eagle* and *Golden Eagle* in 1925. Built by J. Samuel White & Co at its Cowes, Isle of Wight shipyard, she was the first true coastal excursion paddle steamer — as distinct from those built for cross-Channel and Irish Sea services — to exceed 1,000 gross tons, measuring precisely 1,110 tons. The *Crested Eagle* was 309ft (94.2m) long, 34ft 6in (10.5m) in beam over her paddle sponsons and could comfortably carry 1,700

passengers. Oil-fired triple-expansion diagonal engines gave a service speed of 18 knots. She was fitted with a telescopic funnel and a hinged mast, allowing her to pass under the Thames bridges.

Seven years later, the very similar though slightly slower *Royal Eagle* entered service, the largest and most luxurious paddle steamer on the Thames. Her construction had been entrusted to Cammell Laird at Birkenhead. She measured 1,538 gross tons, rivalling the size of the new motor vessels and turbine steamers then being built for the cross-Channel services, and was 292ft (89m) in overall length, with a beam of 37ft (11.2m).

The *Eagle* was disposed of in 1928, but the three remaining General Steam Navigation steamers dominated the Thames

General Steam Navigation's *Golden Eagle*, the only pre-WW1 paddler retained in the fleet after 1928. *Maritime Photo Library*

▲ During her trial runs in the Solent, the *Crested Eagle* shows why she earned the name 'Greyhound of the River'. Her telescopic funnel can be seen to good advantage in this broadside view.
Cowes Maritime Museum

◄ The launch of the *Crested Eagle* at East Cowes, Isle of Wight, on 26 March 1920.
Cowes Maritime Museum

The *Royal Eagle* passes London's commercial docks during another Thames cruise. Unlike the *Crested Eagle,* her funnel was not retractable.
R. C. Riley Collection

▲

General Steam Navigation published a commemorative brochure for the *Royal Eagle's* cruise to Southampton to witness the maiden departure of the *Queen Mary* on 27 May 1936.

▶

A Special One-Day Cruise
BY THE MAGNIFICENT PLEASURE STEAMER
"ROYAL EAGLE"
to witness the undocking of the "QUEEN MARY" and to accompany her down to Spithead and the open sea, on the occasion of her Maiden Voyage to New York,
WEDNESDAY, MAY 27th, 1936
(weather and other circumstances permitting)

R.M.S. "QUEEN MARY"

P.S. "ROYAL EAGLE"

THE *ROYAL EAGLE* is an ideal one-day cruise steamer, having a glass-enclosed lounge on the main deck over 150 feet in length with large windows. Furnished with comfortable chairs and plenty of small tables. This lounge makes passengers independent of the weather. Above is a SUN DECK nearly half the length of the ship. All decks are very spacious and afford every passenger on board an uninterrupted view. An efficient catering service is maintained in bright airy dining saloons. Both the dining saloons and deck lounge have large windows, giving a view of all that passes as the passengers sit in comfort.

THE GENERAL STEAM NAVIGATION CO., LTD.,
15 TRINITY SQUARE, LONDON, E.C.3
TEL.: ROYAL 3200. OR AGENTS.

scene in the inter-war period, the *Royal Eagle* rightly as the fleet's flagship. Their huge capacities allowed them to carry many thousands of passengers each season, generating a good profit for their owners. A distinctive feature of all three, each being single-funnelled, was that the tops of the funnels were cut horizontally rather than angled downwards towards the stern.

The only other new ship to enter the Thames Estuary excursion services between the World Wars was the 318-gross-ton *Medway Queen*, completed in 1924 for the New Medway Steam Packet Co. This concern had been restyled, with the addition of 'New' to its name following its acquisition in 1918 by Captain Shippick, a master mariner with enormous practical experience with paddle vessels. One of the most elegant little steamers placed on the service from

the Medway towns to Southend-on-Sea, the *Medway Queen* was an instant success. She was loved by all who travelled aboard her, and the extra turn of speed of which she was capable permitted the route to be lengthened, with calls out and back at Herne Bay.

A few years later, further additions were made to the New Medway fleet when two former naval paddle minesweepers were purchased for conversion to run the Calais, Boulogne and Dieppe service, each trip commencing from Gravesend with calls *en route* at Clacton and Margate. His Majesty's Ships *Atherstone* and *Melton*, both built in 1916 — *Atherstone* by W. Hamilton, Port Glasgow and *Melton* by Ailsa Shipbuilding Co, Troon — but laid up after World War 1, were purchased from the Admiralty in 1928 and 1929 respectively, the latter

The *Royal Eagle* alongside her terminus at the other end of the Thames, Southend Pier — the longest such structure in the country. Completed originally in 1830 and progressively enlarged, it was reconstructed in iron in 1889 when the electric tramway was added. *Southend Borough Council*

having been already condemned to the shipbreakers. Converted for passenger work, the *Atherstone* commenced excursion cruise service as the *Queen of Kent* in June 1928. The *Queen of Thanet* (ex-*Melton*) joined her a year later. They had a gross tonnage of approximately 795 and their dimensions were 235ft (71.6m) length and 29ft (8.8m) across the beam. Compound diagonal engines gave them a reasonable turn of speed for the long-distance cross-Channel run. They also made cruises to Southend-on-Sea, Great Yarmouth and Sheerness.

Distinctive vessels, the *Queen of Kent* and *Queen of Thanet* had cruiser sterns, full-length promenade decks and two widely-spaced, tall, slim funnels, positioned either side of their paddle boxes. The pair worked these itineraries until 1938 but remained idle during the 1939 season due to the emergence of larger motor vessels on the cross-Channel routes. On the outbreak of World War 2 they were reactivated for a return to auxiliary duties.

World War 1 had had an adverse effect on the financial prosperity of the third big player on the Thames excursion routes, the Coast Development Corporation — operator of the Belle Steamers fleet — which finally went into liquidation in 1929. Over a period of just 10 years, between 1890 and 1900, the company had built seven new steamers, all to Denny Bros designs. Instantly recognisable as consorts, they were now, as a result of the collapse, put on the market. The youngest ship, the *Southwold Belle*, went to French owners while the *Southend Belle* was purchased by the owners of Clacton Pier and continued running under the new name *Laguna Belle*, remaining a favourite on the East Coast. The two oldest vessels, *Clacton Belle* and *London Belle*, were both sold for scrapping. Queen Line, as the New Medway Steam Packet Co was popularly known, acquired the remaining three vessels of the Belle Steamers fleet, continuing to operate them under new identities. The *Woolwich Belle* became the *Queen of the South*, the

The sprightly *Medway Queen*, introduced by the New Medway Steam Packet in 1924. *P&O*

The former Royal Navy minesweeper HMS *Atherstone* entered service on the Thames–Calais/Boulogne services in 1928 as the *Queen of Kent*. Her sister was the *Queen of Thanet* (ex-HMS *Melton*). *World Ship Society*

Originally the *Yarmouth Belle*, the *Queen of Southend*, as shown here, eventually became the *Thames Queen*. She remained on the Gravesend–Southend/Clacton route while employed by the New Medway Steam Packet. *P&O*

x

The *Medway Queen* at Herne Bay on 8 September 1963, as the curtains were about to come down on her long career sailing between the Medway, the Thanet ports and Southend-on-Sea.
John Edgington

Last of the pre-World War 2 paddle steamers, the *Lincoln Castle*, in a view taken in August 1975. Apart from making regular Humber crossings, she was chartered for cruises on the Trent as well as to Goole and Grimsby, a role previously filled by the old steamer *Bilsdale* from 1924 to 1934.
World Ship Society – 4767

The freshly painted paddle box of the *Medway Queen*, photographed while she was undergoing restoration in Kent. *Tom Lee*

▼ *Walton Belle* was renamed *Essex Queen* and the *Yarmouth Belle* was first re-christened as the *Queen of Southend* but was later renamed again, becoming the *Thames Queen*. The former *Woolwich Belle* continued in service until 1932, when she too was sold, to be broken up.

The *Essex Queen*, *Thames Queen* and *Laguna Belle* survived World War 2, performing wartime duties as auxiliary minesweepers or anti-aircraft vessels; the *Essex Queen* also served briefly as a hospital ship. The Belle Steamers company, having brought so much pleasure to East Coast trippers, finally disappeared altogether in 1931 as a consequence of the financial disarray it had suffered.

Later in the 1930s, General Steam Navigation gained a controlling interest in the New Medway Steam Packet Co. Although both fleets retained their unique identities and the ships continued to sail under their respective house flags and in their distinctive liveries, they were marketed as the Eagle & Queen Line from that time, the one company serving the river traffic, the other the estuary trade.

Before turning to the exploits of the coastal paddle vessels during World War 2, mention should be made of the evolving paddle-ferry operations further north on the East Coast, across the River Humber. Again, this was a trade that called for a particular design of small paddle ship. Sturdy and workman-like, with a good reserve of power to handle the strong tidal movements along the river and the vagaries of the weather throughout an all-year-round service, the result was not the most attractive of the coastal paddle steamer designs. Characteristic to them was a large, open area on the main deck aft, used for the carriage of crated cargo, motor vehicles and even livestock.

The *Wingfield Castle*, introduced on the New Holland ferry service in 1934 and latterly operated for British Railways by Associated Humber Lines. *Ian Allan Library*

Run by the LNER since the railway Grouping in 1923, the route from New Holland to Hull benefited between the wars from investment in two quality new ships, first supplementing and then replacing, in part, the older *Cleethorpes, Brocklesby, Killingholme* and *Frodingham*. A third, slightly larger vessel of the new type, the *Lincoln Castle*, was not completed until after the outbreak of war.

First out, in 1934, were the sister ships *Tattershall Castle* and *Wingfield Castle*. Built at West Hartlepool by the yard of William Gray & Co, they had a gross tonnage of 556 and measured 210ft (64.0m) in length and 33ft (10.1m) across the beam. They were not fast vessels, speed not being an essential of this short river crossing. Triple diagonal engines, coal-fired, gave them a maximum speed of 13.5 knots and service speed of 10 knots — adequate for the regular ferry crossings.

The *Tattershall Castle* and *Wingfield Castle* were not confined to a pure scheduled-service role, however. In the late 1930s these Humber ferries also operated a programme of seasonal cruises, taking passengers out around Spurn Head and along the Yorkshire and Lincolnshire coasts to Withernsea and Scarborough or to Cleethorpes. All in all, they were very successful ships, a level of performance that encouraged the construction of a third vessel, having the effect, simultaneously, of deferring plans to construct a long-mooted bridge across the Humber.

Last of the trio, the *Lincoln Castle* — larger than her half-sisters, at 597 gross tons — was launched at the Inglis yard in Glasgow on 29 April 1940. She entered service in August 1941 after making the delivery trip around the north of Scotland in a coastal convoy.

One of the last of the Williamson & Buchanan
steamers, the *Queen Empress* painted navy grey
for the second time in her life, while performing
duties as an auxiliary minesweeper.
Imperial War Museum — A13765

▲

Cosens' *Emperor of India* (ex-*Princess Royal*) serving
as a minesweeper during World War 2. Compare
this with her postwar appearance on page 71.
Imperial War Museum — A13770

▶

3. IN THE SERVICE OF THE NATION

Just as they had been back in 1914, so it was, on the outbreak of World War 2, that the majority of the coastal paddle steamers were requisitioned for auxiliary duties. Initial employment again took the form of coastal minesweeping, their excellent manœuvrability in shallow water suiting this work. By early 1940 five flotillas had been assembled:

7th Minesweeping Flotilla (Rosyth)	7 vessels
8th Minesweeping Flotilla (North Shields)	5 vessels
10th Minesweeping Flotilla (Dover)	8 vessels
11th Minesweeping Flotilla (Greenock)	5 vessels
12th Minesweeping Flotilla (Harwich)	5 vessels

To these 30 paddle minesweepers were added the Southern Railway's *Whippingham* in 1941, by which time the flotilla sizes had been reduced by casualties sustained during the evacuation of the British Expeditionary Forces from the beaches of Dunkirk.

Paddle minesweepers were generally (but not always) attached to flotillas based close to their peacetime regions of operation. For instance, the *Caledonia*, renamed *Goatfell*, and the *Jupiter*, renamed *Scawfell*, were attached to the 11th Flotilla; Southern Railway, Red Funnel and P. & A. Campbell vessels tended to go to the Dover and Harwich stations. As the war progressed, though, and other, more complex roles were devised for the called-up paddle vessels, their duties took them further afield. The *Talisman*, commissioned as HMS *Aristocrat*, supported the unsuccessful amphibious assault on Dieppe in August 1942 and, later, was present in the North African invasion force. Having established her credentials as an amphibious support ship, she became Headquarters Ship for the Mulberry Harbour at Arromanches during Operation 'Neptune' — part of the Normandy Landings — in June 1944. The *Talisman* survived damage caused by enemy gunfire to conclude a creditable war campaign by joining the first convoy into Antwerp after its liberation, delivering relief supplies to the impoverished city.

A marked diversion from previous practice, where vessels of this type were concerned, was to engage them in the thick of the action, directly exposed to the enemy's threat. Nowhere was this demonstrated more than at the evacuation of Dunkirk in 1940. The valiant contribution of the little paddlers, taking advantage of their shallow draft to work close inshore, despite the many risks they confronted, remains a lasting testimony to the Dunkirk spirit. Remembered for the part played by the armada of 'little ships' — the lifeboats, yachts, barges and motorboats, besides the paddle steamers and other coastal ships — the relief of Dunkirk was an incredible feat of national effort, a hugely positive achievement on the brink of calamity that lifted depressed British spirits during some of the darkest days of World War 2.

In all, 25 small coastal paddlers participated in the rescue exercise codenamed Operation 'Dynamo', eight of them P. & A. Campbell vessels — the greatest fleet representation of all. Red Funnel and the Southern Railway contributed four and three of their vessels respectively, while all three of General Steam Navigation's front-line ships were present. Both LNER and the New Medway Steam Packet had two of their craft in the rescue fleet, the *Medway Queen* making no fewer than seven round trips during the emergency.

From 27 May 1940, when the rescue mission was launched, to 5 June, when it was finally broken off, as complete as it could ever be, the paddle steamers worked relentlessly, loading their precious human cargoes and delivering them safely to harbours in Kent and Essex. However, the balance of probabilities dictated that, in performing such perilous work, exposed to shore batteries and enemy aircraft and submarines, there were bound to be casualties. And there were, including some of the latest and best-loved vessels of the excursion fleet.

The first casualty was the *Brighton Belle* (ex-*Lady Evelyn*, built 1900) on 28 May — a loss not caused directly by enemy action. During the return leg of her first crossing to the beaches, she struck a submerged wreck in the 'Downs' and sank.

Her troops and crew transferred to the *Medway Queen* and the *Sandown*, which had been homeward-bound along with the *Brighton Belle*.

The following day's efforts cost three more paddlers. The ever-popular Thames steamer *Crested Eagle*, caught in the open off the Dunkirk beaches, was bombed by German aircraft. Set ablaze, she was run ashore in an attempt to disgorge her crew and the 600 troops she had loaded, but over 300 of those aboard her were either killed or drowned. The four-year-old *Gracie Fields* fell another victim of the marauding German warplanes, as the tempo of the drama on the beach-head continued to intensify. With her engine room damaged and her rudder out of action, all attempts to tow her home were unsuccessful. She sank during the night, but only after her entire complement of soldiers and crew had been taken off safely. Another sad loss was the 41-year-old Clyde steamer *Waverley* which had previously been attached to the 12th Minesweeping Flotilla at Harwich. Having arrived for the first time off the Dunkirk beaches that very day, she managed to take aboard some 600 to 700 troops, despite coming under heavy air attack. On the return crossing she remained the target of continuing attacks from enemy aircraft and was disabled by a bomb-hit when some 15 miles from the French coast. With her steering gear jammed she was left unmanageable, unable to zig-zag and a sitting duck with her rescued troops exposed to enemy fire. As numerous warplanes moved in to finish her off, raining bombs down upon her, the order was given to abandon ship. The *Golden Eagle* and nearby tugs came to the rescue, but the *Waverley* sank so rapidly that it was impossible to save everyone aboard her, and some 350 men lost their lives.

The next 24 hours saw a brief respite from further losses to the paddle fleet, if not from the frenzied rescue effort and the mounting enemy offensive. The following day, 31 May, saw the loss of P. & A. Campbell's *Devonia*, the fifth paddle-steamer casualty of the operation. German bombing attacks left her so severely damaged that she had to be beached and abandoned. Her fleet-mate, the *Brighton Queen* (1905), was sunk the very

Victim of the Dunkirk evacuation, the *Devonia* was beached to prevent her from sinking. In the wake of the exodus of BEF troops, Wehrmacht personnel are photographed in front of the wreck, no doubt to show her off to their families as one of their spoils of war. *Imperial War Museum — HU72101*

next day — the third P. & A. Campbell loss — another victim of German gunfire as enemy shore units closed in on Dunkirk.

A relieved British public welcomed the Government's broadcast on 5 June 1940 announcing that the evacuation of Dunkirk had been brought to a successful conclusion, permitting Great Britain to continue to resist the Nazi war machine. A total of 309,739 British and Allied troops had been rescued and the 25 paddle steamers at Dunkirk (listed in Appendix 1) had accounted for a sizeable share of this number. Though they represented barely 3% of the rescue force, allowing for the fact that many of the other rescue vessels were much smaller, they had saved more than 28,000 lives — around 9% of all the troops evacuated. It had been a David-sized presence but a Goliath-sized contribution. Indeed, it was one of the paddlers, the *Whippingham*, that won acclaim for rescuing the greatest number of troops in a single voyage when she transported 2,700 troops into Dover on 1 June, the sixth day of the evacuation. She was so heavily loaded that she had been in constant danger of capsizing during the Channel crossing.

Sadly, due to later war losses, premature disposals and the state of advanced deterioration of the (by then) two surviving paddle veterans of Dunkirk, none was able to participate in either the 50th or 60th anniversary celebrations of the evacuation. Nor, yet, have either of the survivors — the *Princess Elizabeth* and the *Medway Queen* — been selected for publicly-funded preservation as a lasting national memorial to those epic events of the summer of 1940.

Apart from the sinkings, a number of the other paddlers at Dunkirk had sustained damage, and the auxiliary minesweeping force was somewhat depleted when they resumed these comparatively mundane duties.

From late 1940 through into 1942, the paddle auxiliaries were gradually transferred to new duties, and by January 1943 the minesweeping flotillas had been reduced to just one (the 7th) based at Granton, comprising three active vessels and two others engaged in a training role.

Some paddle steamers, like the *Duchess of Rothesay* (1894), the *Eagle III*, (as HMS *Oriole*) and the *Bournemouth Queen*, became accommodation ships, the latter at Fort William on Scotland's west coast. The *Kylemore* (1897) was converted into a netlayer, and the *Essex Queen* spent three years as a hospital ship. The majority became Auxiliary Anti-Aircraft Vessels — 'Eagle' or 'Ack-Ack' ships, as they were known — based in such diverse locations as Milford Haven, Dover and on the Thames in the heart of London during the Blitz and, later, spotting 'doodlebugs' (V1 pilotless flying bombs) launched from sites in northeast France. Later, these same duties were performed in the Channel, off Normandy, supporting the invasion forces and, as the Allied armies advanced, in the River Scheldt.

▲ The auxiliary paddle minesweepers were converted into Anti-Aircraft Ships as the nature of the German threat changed. This is the *Thames Queen* (the former Belle Steamer *Yarmouth Belle*) equipped for this role. *Imperial War Museum — A13954*

Auxiliary Anti-Aircraft Ships, like the Southern Railway's *Ryde*, provided valuable support during the Normandy invasion, helping to prevent enemy aircraft from attacking the troops on the exposed beach-heads. *Imperial War Museum HU1261*

Although she remained on the 'Home Front' throughout the war, the *Lucy Ashton* was painted navy grey and had anti-aircraft armament mounted as a protection against patrolling German aircraft. The photograph, taken on 16 February 1943, was released by the LNER after the war's end. *Ian Allan Library*

Before we leave the minesweepers' story, there were also losses sustained while performing these vital but unglamorous duties which deserve to be mentioned here. The first was Caledonia Steam Packet's six-year-old *Mercury*, which sank off Southern Ireland after striking a mine on 26 December 1940. Another relatively new vessel, Southern Railway's *Southsea*, suffered a similar fate on 16 February 1941 when she struck a mine in the mouth of the Tyne, off South Shields. She was beached and abandoned, seven of her crew being killed in the incident. Three other auxiliary paddle minesweepers fell victim to enemy bombing, the *Marmion* (1906) off Harwich during the night of 9 April 1941, the *City of Rochester* (1904) while berthed at Chatham on 19 May 1941 and P. & A. Campbell's *Barry* (ex-*Waverley*), under the name *Snaefell*, in the entrance to the River Tyne on 5 July 1941. Although the wreck of the *Marmion* was subsequently raised, she was declared unfit for further service.

Only two paddle steamers were lost while in service as Auxiliary Anti-Aircraft Vessels. The LMS's new *Juno*, operating under the temporary naval name *Helvellyn*, was bombed and sunk on 20 March 1941 while lying in the London Docks along with her sister *Jupiter*, both then operating as units of the Thames Defence Flotilla. She was declared to be a constructive total loss. Three years later, on 2 September 1944, P. & A. Campbell suffered its fifth casualty of the conflict when the *Glen Avon* foundered off the coast of Normandy while supporting the Allied invasion forces.

Two other paddlers performed vital roles in connection with the Allies' D-Day invasion of Normandy. The New Medway Steam Packet vessels *Queen of Kent* (ex-HMS *Atherstone*) and

▲ War service over, the *Royal Eagle* is temporarily laid up awaiting return to her owners, with a Royal Navy paddle tug beyond her.
Imperial War Museum — A1806

Queen of Thanet (ex-HMS *Melton*) were employed as Control Ships responsible for the assembly and despatch of Mulberry Harbour units. Located respectively off Dungeness, Kent, and Selsey, Sussex, they also provided accommodation for the 'Phoenix' and 'Whale' handling parties.

Meanwhile, for those paddle steamers left on the home front continuing to maintain essential ferry services, life was not exactly cosy. As a measure of the arduous demands placed upon them, the *Lucy Ashton*'s wartime career is typical. She was retained to sustain the Clyde ferry single-handed from September 1939 to May 1945. During this time she steamed 143,297 miles and carried 1,128,258 passengers. And these commercial duties were not without their risks, either, for the threat of enemy aircraft or mine was just as potent as it was for those vessels that had been called up for the duration. While crossing from Portsmouth to Ryde in the early hours of

20 September 1941, Southern Railway's *Portsdown* was blown up by a mine and sunk. Earlier, during an air raid on Southampton in December 1940, the *Duchess of Cornwall* (ex *Duchess of York*) and *Her Majesty* were sunk at the Royal Pier. The *Duchess of Cornwall* was salvaged and, after repairs, returned to Red Funnel's passage service, but *Her Majesty*, damaged beyond recovery, was subsequently scrapped.

One of the more unusual but extremely beneficial contributions to the war effort was that made by the small Loch Lomond steamers *Princess May* and *Prince Edward*. Effectively land-locked, they were unable, therefore, to perform auxiliary service, although they were probably too small to have had much military value anyway. Instead they provided temporary accommodation for Clydeside families whose homes had been bombed during the German air raids.

An equally resourceful utilisation of the Thames excursion fleet back in 1939, immediately prior to the outbreak of war, saw them involved in the evacuation of children from Greater London to the relative safety of Suffolk and Norfolk. The *Royal Eagle*, *Crested Eagle*, *Golden Eagle*, *Medway Queen* and *Laguna Belle*, along with the motor vessels *Royal Daffodil*, *Royal Sovereign* and *Queen of the Channel*, carried nearly 20,000 schoolchildren from the perceived danger area of Gravesend, Dagenham and Tilbury out to Felixstowe, Lowestoft and Great Yarmouth.

When the war was finally over, the national paddle-steamer fleet had diminished by the 13 vessels that had been sunk. Besides these losses, many of the remaining ships, especially the older ones, had been worn out by the strenuous service they had been called upon to perform. The years ahead were destined to be a period of departures (numerous) and arrivals (few), as many of these veteran paddlers were retired and new vessels took their place.

4. POSTWAR REVIVAL

With the cessation of hostilities in Europe from May 1945, the Admiralty progressively returned the requisitioned paddle steamers for commercial service. Many were in a sad and sorry state, though, being no longer fit to resume pleasure cruises or ferry duties. It seems ironic that, having survived the war, many soon fell victim to the cutter's torch; however, as renovation was not viable in most cases, condemnation to the scrapyard was the only realistic option. By the close of the 1940s, no fewer than 12 paddlers had suffered this fate, many admittedly in advanced years.

P. & A. Campbell's *Cambria* and *Westward Ho* were early casualties of the demolition process, although their sister ship *Britannia* survived for another 10 years. The last of the once famous Williamson & Buchanan steamers of the River Clyde sadly disappeared for ever with the premature disposal of the *Queen Empress* and *Eagle III*. Equally, the need to retire three of Red Funnel's front-line ships, the *Balmoral*, *Lorna Doone* and *Solent Queen*, was accepted with great reluctance.

Though expensive to run, the *Balmoral* had in her time been a great standard-bearer for the company and a worthy rival to Campbell's *Cambria* for speed honours. Her fate was decided after she had languished for two years in a mud berth on the River Itchen. The old *Lorna Doone*, which had been in the company's employ since 1898, was regarded as one of the most successful excursion vessels. Laid up at Northam, Southampton, on her return from the Admiralty, in October 1948 she was moved to the nearby Pollock Brown breaker's yard and broken up for scrap. Similarly, the slightly older *Solent Queen*, Red Funnel's last iron-hulled steamer, was sold for breaking-up by Thomas Ward at Grays, Essex, after she suffered boiler failure in August 1948. As a token reminder of the days of the 'butterfly boats', as the paddlers were affectionately termed by deep-sea merchant seamen, her binnacle has been retained on display at the National Maritime Museum.

When one considers the ages that some of these paddle

◄ In London & North Eastern Railway (originally North British) colours postwar, the classic Clyde paddle steamer *Jeanie Deans*. She is seen on a trial run on 31 May 1946, following reconditioning after war service. *Ian Allan Library*

steamers had attained by the time they were demolished — Red Funnel's *Princess Helena* was 69 years old at the end of her career in 1952 — it was a great testimony to the quality of workmanship of the British shipbuilding and marine engineering industry. Most had clocked up over half a century of active service, including arduous auxiliary duties on two occasions. Many were still coal-burning, and the majority still had their original engines.

The last remnants of another paddle steamer institution evaporated in the immediate postwar years with the disposal of the last of the former Belle steamers, albeit under different identities. Once welcome sights along the Thames reach, the *Laguna Belle* and *Thames Queen* passed on in 1948, followed by the *Essex Queen*, sailing latterly as the *Pride of Devon*, in 1951.

Other pleasure steamers were luckier. Despite evident changes (generally of a detrimental nature) in both the ferry and excursion trades, some vessels were fortunate in being transferred to new owners for continued employment, despite their longevity. British Railways, as successor to the Southern Railway, sold its *Shanklin* to Cosens in 1950, the former ferry ending her days as the dedicated cruise vessel *Monarch*, second steamer of the name. Cosens had experienced a change of ownership in 1946 when, in the face of a hostile takeover by a competitor, Red Funnel purchased 70% of the Weymouth company's shares to make it a wholly owned subsidiary. Although under Red Funnel's control, Cosens continued to run its services much as before.

Cosens' second *Monarch*, the ◄ former *Shanklin*, on 20 July 1951. Purchased from British Railways in 1950, she continued making pleasure trips until 1961, when she was sold for breaking-up. *Ian Allan Library*

Berthed at Dunoon, the ► DEPV *Talisman*. To the right, in the tower above the pier building, is an example of the signalling system developed by Charles Allan to control paddle steamer movements at the Clyde piers. *Ian Allan Library*

Red Funnel was again involved when the two substantial Medway excursion paddle steamers *Queen of Kent* and *Queen of Thanet* came onto the market in the winter of 1948/9. After war service, they had briefly been reinstated by the New Medway Steam Packet on estuary cruises from 1947. Bought by Red Funnel two winters later, they were moved to the John I. Thornycroft shipyard on the River Itchen for refit. They emerged in May and June 1949, running day excursions from Bournemouth, reactivating, respectively, the popular names *Lorna Doone* and *Solent Queen*. Planned trips to the Normandy beaches did not take off, but their seasonal summer employment was supplemented when they were chartered by the Royal Southampton Yacht Club for Cowes Regatta Week, the *Solent Queen* in 1949 and the *Lorna Doone* in 1950 and 1951. Red Funnel had commissioned a new motor vessel, the *Balmoral*, in 1949 and clearly had no intention of building new ships with paddle propulsion.

As it turned out, the South Coast careers of the two former naval minesweepers were extremely short-lived, lasting less than three full seasons. The fact was that they were expensive to operate and unprofitable. At the height of the 1950 summer season the *Solent Queen* was blighted with persistent boiler problems, forcing her transfer to the local Ryde service, for which she was ill suited. The following summer, while high and dry on the Whites' shipyard slipway during her annual survey and overhaul, her fate was sealed when her aft end was gutted by fire on 22 June 1951. Those parts of her which had not been destroyed by the flames had been severely damaged by smoke, heat and water, and she was declared a

Rebuilt after war service, the Cosens excursion steamer *Emperor of India* gave her owners 10 seasons of work before she was broken up at Bruges from January 1957. *Ian Allan Library*

The *Lorna Doone* (ex-*Queen of Kent*) passes a Union Castle express mail steamer berthed at Southampton's Old Docks as she makes her way to the terminus at the Royal Pier. This view makes an interesting comparison with the photograph of the same ship as HMS *Atherstone* on page 19. *World Ship Society*

The *Cardiff Queen* alongside the quay at Ilfracombe at low tide on 22 May 1959. With her near-sister *Bristol Queen* she gave her owner 20 years of good service. *R. C. Riley* ▲

At Cardiff in 1964, the *Bristol Queen* was the largest paddle steamer owned by P. & A. Campbell. Efforts to retain her as a memorial to the great age of the pleasure steamers in the Bristol Channel were in vain. *John Edgington* ▶

constructive total loss. It was hinted that Red Funnel retained aspirations to restore her, but she nevertheless went to Dover breakers that October. It was as if her loss hastened the demise of the *Lorna Doone*, for, while the latter was undergoing her next closed-season overhaul in January 1952, the order was given to abandon all work on her, and she was returned to lay up in her winter mud berth. Two months later she too was towed to Dover for breaking-up. Thus ended the careers of two striking paddle ships which had never completely fulfilled expectations, either as naval or as merchant vessels.

Elsewhere, new ships were being commissioned, albeit only in very limited numbers. Most ambitious was the large pair of paddle pleasure steamers introduced by P. & A. Campbell for its West Country operations. Entering service in 1946, the *Bristol Queen* was built locally by Charles Hill & Sons, Bristol, while, for the slightly smaller *Cardiff Queen*, introduced in 1947, P. & A. Campbell went to the Fairfield shipyard on the Clyde. Displaying a clear 'family' resemblance with earlier White Funnel ships, the *Bristol Queen* and *Cardiff Queen* were among the most pleasing paddle steamers to behold, having a balanced profile topped by twin-cowled funnels — a feature fitted as standard to P. & A. Campbell's fleet. At 765 gross tons, the *Cardiff Queen* measured 248ft (75.6m) in length and 30ft (9.1m) across the beam; equivalent dimensions for the 961-gross-ton *Bristol Queen* were 258ft (78.7m) and 31ft (9.5m). Steam-reciprocating, triple-expansion oil-fired engines gave both vessels a speed of 16.5 knots.

▲ Comings and goings at Penarth pier on 20 April 1957: the second of P. & A. Campbell's new postwar-built steamers, the *Cardiff Queen*, arriving while *en route* to Weston-super-Mare, and …

◄ … the marginally larger *Bristol Queen*, leaving for Minehead. The *Bristol Queen* was the first paddle-propelled vessel to be built in Bristol since 1854.
(both) Ian Allan Library

In 1948, as promised, the new Labour Government had launched the nationalised British Railways, amalgamating the operations of the 'Big Four' railway companies under a single authority. With the exception of those of the Clyde region, this had little effect on the railway-run ferry operations around the British Isles, apart from a change of ownership. On the Clyde, the former LNER and LMS vessels were combined into a single fleet run by the Caledonian Steam Packet, which now maintained the services for the Scottish Region of British Railways. Prior to the amalgamation, the LNER had ordered what would turn out to be the last Clyde paddler, reviving the name of the ship lost at Dunkirk, seven years earlier, which had been probably the most popular boat in the Clyde fleet of 1939. The new 693-gross-ton *Waverley* entered service in 1947 but was fated to wear LNER colours, originally those of the

The new *Waverley* at Rothesay. The renewed hope for the steamer trades that she and the P. & A. Campbell near-sisters represented was, unfortunately, short-lived, declining rapidly through the 1960s. *Ian Allan Library*

▶ The small river paddler *Alumchine* at Neyland on 31 July 1951. One of the smallest paddle ferries ever operated in the United Kingdom, measuring just 76 tons gross, she maintained regular crossings of Milford Haven from 1947 to 1956. Built in 1923 at Queensferry, Cheshire, she was permitted by her passenger certificate to carry a maximum of 216 persons, but could also convey cattle and cars. Later, a new ferry, the *Cleddau Queen* — the last UK-built paddle steamer — was placed on the service. *R. C. Riley*

North British Railway, for just one season. A year later, along with the other vessels of the combined Clyde fleet, she adopted the yellow funnel with black top of her nationalised owners. Built by A. & J. Inglis at Pointhouse, Glasgow, the *Waverley* was 248ft (75.6m) long and 30ft (9.1m) across her beam.

It seems that it was only on the Clyde Estuary and in the Bristol Channel that there was sufficient confidence to embark upon the construction of new paddle vessels. On the River Thames, from as early as the start of the 1950s, craft of this type were already becoming obsolete, displaced by modern-styled motor passenger vessels. General Steam Navigation had received the *Golden Eagle* back from the Admiralty in 1945 and the *Royal Eagle* in the following May. They were refitted at the company's own Deptford workshops, known as 'The Stowage', and immediately returned to the Kent coastal service, the *Royal Eagle* making her first postwar commercial sailing on 8 June 1946. However, the character of the summer

pleasure-cruise scene on the Thames had completely altered, and it was no longer possible to fill the big paddlers.

Laid up in the Medway, the *Golden Eagle* was disposed of for scrap in 1951. The *Royal Eagle*, idle since August 1950, ended her days in like fashion; despite attempts to sell her to another operator or for static use as a maritime training school, she was broken up at Grays, Essex, from January 1954. Her comparative youth — she was only 21 years old — was a hint that the decline of the paddle steamer was accelerating. In just eight years, the Thames/ Medway paddle excursion fleet had been reduced to just one vessel, the *Medway Queen*.

Despite the gloomy outlook, yet another new paddle steamer entered service in this period. Completed in 1953, another product of the A. & J. Inglis shipyard, the *Maid of the Loch*, was the largest and last of the Loch Lomond paddlers; indeed, with dimensions of 208ft (63.4m) in length and 28ft (8.5m) across the beam, she was the largest vessel operating

The *Jeanie Deans*, looking very much at home in the waters of the Scottish lochs. She was one of the most popular of the Clyde steamers, retaining much of the elegant styling of the previous generation of paddle vessels. *Jordan & Pollock, courtesy Tom Lee*

The diesel-electric *Talisman* off Tighnabruaich in August 1964. *John Edgington*

DAY CRUISES TO THE SEA

From TOWER OF LONDON PIER (8.45 a.m.) CALLING AT GREENWICH (9.15 a.m.)
(DAILY EXCEPT FRIDAYS)

P/s ROYAL EAGLE

WHITSUN to MID-SEPTEMBER

	DAY RETURN	
	MON./THUR.	SAT./SUN.
SOUTHEND	6/6	6/6
MARGATE	12/6	16/6
RAMSGATE	13/6	17/6

Apply C.S.N.Cº. LTD. 15. TRINITY SQ. E.C.3. 'phone ROYAL 3200

◀ Another view of the *Waverley*, showing her arriving at Dunoon pier on 22 August 1968 with another excursion steamer approaching in her wake. Even in the late 1960s the cruise schedules on the Clyde remained full, and there was plenty of choice for prospective passengers. *David L. Williams*

The *Royal Eagle* at Tower Bridge, a poster by Harry Hudson Rodmell. The *Royal Eagle* was the first Thames excursion steamer to have a sun deck and sun lounge. *P&O*

Campbell's remaining paddlers had, by the end of the 1950s, been reduced to just two — the modern *Bristol Queen* and *Cardiff Queen*. The *Lady Moyra* and the *Ravenswood*, then 64 years old, were sold for scrap in 1955, the old *Britannia* going the same way in the following year. The *Glen Usk* and *Glen Gower* were withdrawn in 1958 to be broken up in Belgium two years later.

As already noted, paddle steamers had by this time virtually disappeared completely from the Thames, and they were about to make a final departure from Red Funnel's South Coast operations. Following the disposal of the *Princess Helena* in 1952 and the vintage *Lord Elgin* — at 79 years of age, the oldest paddler afloat — the popular excursion vessel *Bournemouth Queen* became yet another casualty in 1955, being broken up at Ghent from January 1958. She had been extensively rebuilt after the war: on her return to service in July 1947 her engines ran on oil fuel, her interiors had been remodelled and permanent metal bulwarks had been erected forward. She had a new, cowled funnel and her wheelhouse had been enclosed. Her new look was completed with the erection of a main mast in 1954 in satisfaction of revised Board of Trade rules. With the passing of the *Bournemouth Queen*, Red Funnel was left with just one paddle steamer — the *Princess Elizabeth* — but she did not survive into the 1960s either.

Only the British Transport Commission (British Railways) retained all its paddle vessels in active operation into the 1960s, these consisting of four vessels on the Spithead ferry service and three on the Eastern Region's Humber crossing. The Southern Region ships had been supplemented with three new screw-driven motor vessels — *Brading*, *Shanklin* and *Southsea* — introduced between 1948 and 1951. At that time the Portsmouth–Ryde and Yarmouth–Lymington routes, benefiting from the bumper traffic of the 1950s, when the Isle of Wight was among the most popular resort destinations in the country, could comfortably support seven ships. It was reported that,

on Britain's inland waterways. Too big to enter the loch by way of the narrow channel of the River Leven, she was transported in sections by rail and assembled at Balloch, her home port.

The various comings, of which there were few, and goings, of which there were many more, had substantially reduced the paddle steamers' numbers by the late 1950s compared with their prewar level. Disposal of the *Lucy Ashton*, in 1951, the *Duchess of Fife*, in 1953, and the *Marchioness of Lorne* (just 20 years old), in 1955, had reduced the strength of the Clyde region paddle fleet to just five vessels, plus the new *Maid of the Loch*. Similarly, P. & A.

on typical Saturdays during the summer months, as many as 3,000 passengers an hour were arriving at Ryde pierhead, with an equivalent number returning to the mainland.

The decade of the 1950s was realistically the swansong era of the coastal excursion paddle steamer. For many, this was almost the last opportunity to experience a carefree coastal trip. Cruises aboard these unique vessels hung on through the next decade but on a much reduced scale. To their credit, despite waning popularity and diminishing returns, the operators made every effort to maintain their vessels in tip-top condition, lavishing attention on their furnishings and paintwork. Although it was not appreciated at the time, this was the start of the modern age, in which faster and more exotic thrills were becoming the vogue. Regrettably, the joys of a lazy afternoon on the water, soaking in the sunshine and bracing sea air or hanging over the rail watching the churning wake of the mighty paddle wheels, were increasingly becoming a dimension of the past.

▲ The *Bournemouth Queen* was substantially rebuilt after World War 2, but stability problems led to her having to operate under restricted certification from 1951 onwards. *Red Funnel Group*

◄ After the retirement of the *Bournemouth Queen* on 29 August 1957, the *Princess Elizabeth* took over her cruise programme, becoming the last Red Funnel vessel to operate from Bournemouth. Here she is alongside Southampton's Royal Pier, loading cars and passengers for the crossing to Cowes. *Maritime Photo Library*

An atmospheric scene at Tarbet, Loch Lomond, in August 1968, showing the *Maid of the Loch* embarking passengers for the return run to Balloch. The *Maid of the Loch* was and still is the largest excursion vessel ever to operate on Loch Lomond or British inland waterways as a whole.
David L. Williams

The pleasures of a Clyde excursion trip often included musical entertainment. Another delight, as recalled by the author, were the very tasty Scotch Pancakes that could be purchased in the on-board dining saloons.
David L. Williams

The Naval Review at Spithead in Coronation year, in June 1953, made a marvellous spectacle for the South Coast excursion fleet. Here Red Funnel is promoting one of the many cruises to view the anchored ships, in this case aboard the *Bournemouth Queen*.

The *Ryde* at Newhaven on 12 May 1968. *John Edgington*

In the King George V graving dock at Southampton — a facility originally constructed for the much larger Cunard 'Queens' — British Railways' *Sandown* shows off her underwater hull during an overhaul in May 1963. Her bow rudder can be clearly seen. *Ray Sprake*

5. DECLINE AND PRESERVATION

Viewed in retrospect, the transitional years of the 1960s were a time of rapid technological advancement and a period when established patterns of social behaviour and aspirations were in the throes of far-reaching and radical change. Partly as a consequence, it was a period that also witnessed the displacement of many traditional forms of transport. The private-transport revolution was about to explode as Dr Beeching's cuts carved up the railways. Television had opened up the world at large, enticing an increasingly adventurous population to sample the pleasures of foreign lands through affordable package holidays, travelling by jet aircraft. As the piers and beaches in this country emptied, so

too the queues of passengers for excursion trips shortened until, with mounting losses, they were no longer viable to operate. It was the same for ferry crossings, which had rapidly to adapt to cater for the growing number of motor cars. The older ships, designed primarily for foot passengers, were progressively replaced with specialised vehicle-carrying vessels.

The impact of these changes was swift and unremitting. As the 1960s advanced, paddle-steamer operations were wound down, although, in truth, they clung on to the very last all around the coast. Sad to say, little can be recorded of this period other than the fates of those few remaining paddle ships and the efforts made in each case to spare them

The *Jupiter* survived into the 1960s, but only just, and then only to cross to Dublin for breaking after a long spell of inactivity at Greenock. *Ian Allan Library*

from oblivion once 'Finished with engines' had been rung on their engine-room telegraph for the very last time. It is a story of mixed fortunes.

Recognising that this unique form of water transportation was fast disappearing, the Paddle Steamer Preservation Society (originally the Paddle Steamer Trust) was founded in 1959 by Professor Alan Robinson in a bid to save as many of these wonderful craft as possible. It was a timely intervention, for, in just a very few years, little would be left fit for preservation. In the event, along with other associated groups, the Society has been successful in rescuing, for the pleasure of future generations, a small number of paddle steamers, two of which are in full operational order. The Society's most famous personality and long-time patron was the late Poet Laureate, Sir John Betjeman.

On the Clyde, the *Jupiter*, which had been withdrawn from service back in the autumn of 1957, became the first casualty of the decade. Despite hopes to reactivate her, her long spell of inactivity in the Albert Harbour, Greenock, ended on 6 April 1961, when she made her last trip across the Irish Sea to Dublin, where she was broken up. That same year, Cosens disposed of the old *Monarch*, the one-time Southern Railway ferry *Shanklin*. Another Cosens vessel, paid off at the end of the next season, was the veteran *Consul*, which had been active cruising until the very last.

Changing visitor trends to the Isle of Wight had led to the introduction by British Railways of more roll-on, roll-off car ferries — improved screw-propelled versions of the motor paddle ferry *Farringford* which had entered service in 1947. The change of emphasis caused the displacement of the remaining paddle steamers, beginning with the *Freshwater*, which continued in service for a short time, first as the *Sussex Queen* and then under the name *Swanage Queen*, until events finally overtook her in 1962. She was followed into retirement by the Dunkirk veteran *Whippingham* in 1963. Both were scrapped.

Early in the 1960s the paddle excursions on the River Dart were wound up. Of the three surviving vessels, the *Totnes Castle* was sold for scrap, while the *Compton Castle* and *Kingswear Castle* were both laid up. Defying the unwelcome attentions of the breakers, the *Totnes Castle* sank in the English Channel in 1967 while *en route* to Plymouth — a far more fitting end. The *Compton Castle* remained idle at Kingsbridge, where she was used for the shooting of interior scenes for the television production *The Onedin Line*. Subsequently, she was converted into a floating café and museum. Ordered to be moved from Kingsbridge in April 1979 by South Hamm District Council, she has been relocated in a new lay-up berth in the centre of a road roundabout at Truro. The *Kingswear Castle* benefited from rescue by the Paddle Steamer Preservation Society in 1967 — its first preservation effort. Following a thorough restoration, she is once again running short cruises each summer on the rivers Medway and Thames, based at Strood.

▲ The *Consul* at Lulworth Cove, Dorset, on 10 June 1959, revealing again the rather precarious arrangement for embarking and disembarking passengers. Built as the *Duke of Devonshire*, she passed into Cosens ownership in 1938. *Ian Allan Library*

The *Swanage Queen* (ex-*Freshwater*) berthed in Poole Harbour on 3 July 1961, less recognisable with a blue and black funnel. *R. C. Riley*

The museum-cum-café ship *Compton Castle* laid up in a mud berth in the centre of a busy roundabout at Truro. Her engines are now displayed at the Bembridge Maritime Museum, Isle of Wight. *David Reed — 22930*

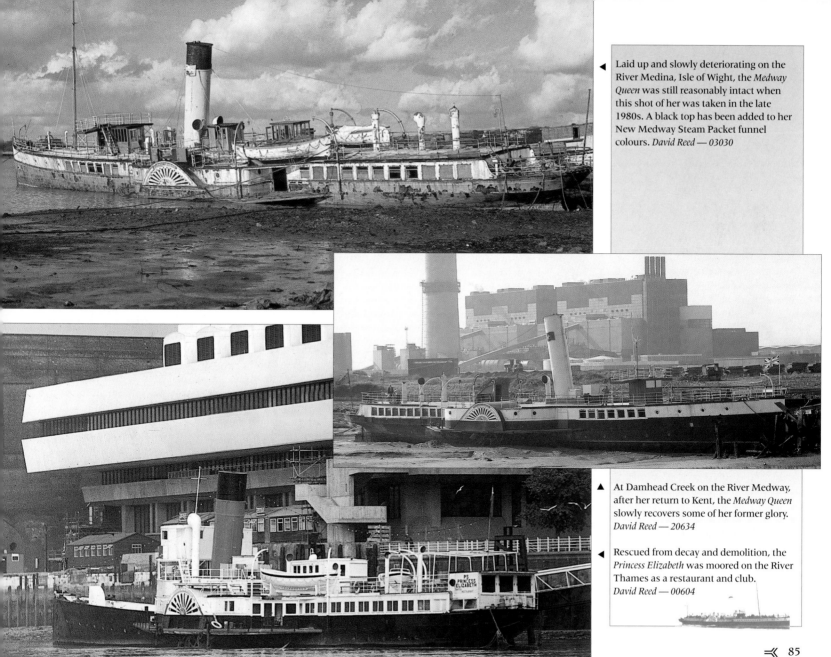

Laid up and slowly deteriorating on the River Medina, Isle of Wight, the *Medway Queen* was still reasonably intact when this shot of her was taken in the late 1980s. A black top has been added to her New Medway Steam Packet funnel colours. *David Reed — 03030*

At Damhead Creek on the River Medway, after her return to Kent, the *Medway Queen* slowly recovers some of her former glory. *David Reed — 20634*

Rescued from decay and demolition, the *Princess Elizabeth* was moored on the River Thames as a restaurant and club. *David Reed — 00604*

relatively sheltered backwater. However, as the years progressed and the initial curiosity of a floating nightspot lost its appeal, she fell into disrepair and was left to deteriorate.

In 1984 the *Medway Queen* was purchased by the Medway Queen Preservation Trust from the liquidators of Wight Marina for the sum of £10,000, in a state almost beyond recovery. A tricky operation to float her onto a salvage pontoon for the return trip to the Medway was accomplished without mishap. Now located on the Hoo peninsula, the *Medway Queen* is undergoing a slow but advancing restoration, although it is extremely unlikely that she will be other than a static exhibit when it is completed. The danger is that, unless the costs to keep her in good order can be recovered from sufficient visitors, she may once again be threatened. If ever a ship deserved to be retained as a national treasure, permanently berthed in a prime location as a memorial to the Dunkirk evacuation, the *Medway Queen* is the one.

Back on the Clyde, the *Jeanie Deans* and the *Talisman* were withdrawn from service at the end of successive seasons in the mid-1960s. The *Jeanie Deans* was purchased and brought south to run summer excursions along the Thames to Southend-on-Sea under the new name *Queen of the South*, which she did in 1966 and 1967. However, failure to attract sufficient fare-paying passengers led to an early suspension of the enterprise, and the 37-year-old paddler was re-sold for breaking-up.

At the end of her Red Funnel days, the old *Princess Elizabeth*, like the *Freshwater*, found continued employment with new owners — a rather fragmented experience that continued until 1966. She undertook a programme of cruises from Torquay for Torbay Steamers in 1960 and 1961, following a thorough refit by the John I. Thornycroft shipyard at Southampton. In 1962 she worked from Bournemouth to Swanage after her owner reformed as Coastal Steamers & Marine Services, a year later relocating at Weymouth, where she continued to make sailings until the end of the 1965 season. Her active career over, the *Princess Elizabeth* was sold to form part of a planned Sussex casino project, but this fell through. Subsequently sold for breaking-up, in October 1967 she was towed to Woolston, where her engines and boilers were removed in preparation for the end. Whatever future

The career of another member of the Dunkirk evacuation fleet, the *Medway Queen*, came to an end in 1963, spelling the end of Medway cruises until the introduction of the restored *Kingswear Castle* in 1984. Destined originally to be broken up in Belgium, two years later the 'Heroine of Dunkirk', as she had been called, was moved instead to the River Medina, on the Isle of Wight, where she was to feature as part of a marina development. She opened as a restaurant and nightclub a year later, and, for a time, at least, her future seemed secure in this

was in prospect, she was condemned from that time to remaining immobile. Although further dubious marina-development plans were announced, the rusting vessel stayed put. Reprieve from this slow decay came in the form of purchase by Don Hickman, who had her extensively refitted to become a restaurant and club moored on the River Thames just below Tower Bridge.

Repainted white with a black-topped white funnel, the *Princess Elizabeth* took up station in June 1970. She remained there for three years, until redevelopment of the St Katherine's Dock area forced a move to a new berth. She then reopened at Queenhithe Dock in 1974, transferring to the Swan Pier in 1975. From 1987 she resided in another European capital, being moored at the Pont Mirabeau on the River Seine in Paris and functioning as an art gallery and conference centre. Since then she has been relocated, appropriately enough, at Dunkirk.

The last two Solent paddlers, *Sandown* and *Ryde*, held on with Wightlink (a division of British Railways) until 1966 and 1969 respectively, both having clocked up over 30 years of service. The *Sandown* was scrapped, but the *Ryde* was sold for retention as the nightclub *Ryde Queen* at the marina complex at Binfield, Isle of Wight, where she joined the *Medway Queen*. All went well for a long period, but she was gutted by fire on 10 August 1977 and has been largely neglected ever since. Locked in her mud berth, she is now in a pitiful condition, realistically beyond recovery. No doubt, at some time the former *Ryde* will be declared a public danger and will be broken up where she lies.

Meanwhile, P. & A. Campbell paid off its remaining two paddlers at the end of the 1968 season, bringing the curtain down on a distinctive presence on the Bristol Channel that had continued unbroken for over three quarters of a century.

Attempts were made to retain the *Bristol Queen* for preservation, but, when these failed, she, like the *Cardiff Queen*, was broken up in Belgium.

The last two Clyde paddle steamers, the *Caledonia* and *Waverley*, were probably destined for a similar fate when they ceased operations, but intervention resulted in a better outcome in both cases, though with varying fortunes.

The *Caledonia*'s final sailing for the Caledonian Steam Packet

The *Ryde* during a rare visit to Southampton in August 1969, when her working career was drawing to a close.
Ray Sprake

The renamed *Ryde Queen* looking superb when she was first berthed on the River Medina as a nightclub and restaurant. Compare this with the view of her opposite. Note that the distinctive opposed-arrows Wightlink logo has been removed from her funnel.
David Reed — 00310

Thirty years after her retirement from active service, the former *Ryde* makes a pitiful sight, slowly disintegrating in her mud berth alongside the River Medina. *David L. Williams*

The *Old Caledonia* on the Thames, following the fire that brought her new function as a floating pub/restaurant to a premature end in 1980. *David Reed — 00550*

her former fleet-mate, the turbine steamer *Queen Mary*.

The *Waverley* passed into CalMac (the shortened name of Caledonian MacBrayne Ltd — the company formed from the merger of the Caledonian Steam Packet with David MacBrayne) ownership from 1973. However, she was declared surplus to the company's requirements, and in the winter of that year she was sold to the Paddle Steamer Preservation Society for the grand sum of £1! The associated company Waverley Steam Navigation Co was formed to run her thenceforward as an active excursion craft, at first solely on the Clyde but latterly on an extended cruise programme all round the British Isles. Today the *Waverley* is the only working example of the coastal excursion paddle steamer.

was on 7 October 1969. She then spent a brief period on the Tarbet mail service, under charter to David MacBrayne, before being sold for breaking-up by Arnott, Young & Co. For some reason she was renamed *Old Caledonia*. Laid up at Dalmuir, awaiting the cutter's torch, she was reprieved at the eleventh hour when Bass Charrington acquired her for conversion into a high-class 'Thirties-style theme restaurant and bar. Resplendent in a new brown, yellow and white livery, she was moored on the Victoria Embankment in London, just above Waterloo Bridge. Her adaptation, under the professional stewardship of this major brewing concern, proved to be a successful venture, sadly ended prematurely when the *Old Caledonia* was severely and irretrievably damaged by a fire in 1980. She has since been replaced by

Long may she continue to operate.

The only other paddle vessel remaining 'north of the Border' was the *Maid of the Loch*, which had also passed into the new Caledonian MacBrayne fleet. She continued to make cruises under the CalMac banner but was never profitable, having been aided by subsidies for much of her life. Now laid up, effectively trapped within Loch Lomond and thus precluding most rescue options, the *Maid of the Loch* faces an uncertain future, although restoration has now commenced.

The last scheduled paddle services were those between Hull and New Holland on the River Humber finally rendered redundant by the opening of the Humber Bridge in 1978. Today the three former paddle ferries constitute a remarkable trio of survivors.

The *Tattershall Castle* was the first to be withdrawn, in 1972. At the time of her withdrawal, it was estimated that, over the course of her 38-year career, she had conveyed 15 million passengers and many thousands of vehicles. Today she is berthed alongside the north bank of the Thames between Charing Cross and Westminster bridges, in the shadow of Big Ben and under the watchful gaze of the 'London Eye'. Following conversion by the Humber Graving Dock at Immingham between July 1973 and December 1975, the *Tattershall Castle* was officially opened as the 'Embankment Gallery' by the Lord Mayor of Westminster on 24 February 1976. Her funnel was shortened for the tow under the Thames bridges. Her triple-expansion engines remain intact, and, for the benefit of visitors, are slowly turned over by an electric motor.

The *Tattershall Castle*'s sister ship, the *Wingfield Castle*, was retired in September 1973, replaced temporarily by the former Isle of Wight car ferry *Farringford*. Subsequently, she languished in London's Royal Albert Docks amid rumours that she was to be moved to San Antonio, Texas (which, incidentally, is inland), crossing the Atlantic under her own steam! Links with dubious marina developments ensued, epitomised by one particular advertisement which offered her for sale for £30,000 as an 'excellent subject for conversion to restaurant, club or pub'. Thankfully, she managed to evade these superficial enterprises, and the *Wingfield Castle* is now back in her birthplace as one of the exhibits in Hartlepool's Municipal Museum, berthed outside the former William Gray shipyard.

Last of the trio, the *Lincoln Castle* was retired in March 1978 after she failed her annual survey because of boiler defects. The Humber Paddle Steamer Group was formed to ensure her preservation. Though their efforts have so far met with limited success, she remains moored at Grimsby, close to the area where she worked for almost 40 years, with reasonable prospects for retention and restoration over the longer term.

Few vestiges of the once immense fleet of British coastal paddle steamers now remain. There are the active *Waverley* and *Kingswear Castle*, the static *Princess Elizabeth*, *Compton Castle*, *Medway Queen* and *Ryde Queen*, plus the *Tattershall Castle*, *Wingfield Castle* and *Lincoln Castle*, along with a number of decorative paddle boxes, engine parts and other items of paddle steamer ephemera. In themselves, they still capture much of the splendour of that magnificent era of coastal passenger shipping and should not be missed by those with a passion for these craft. It is hoped also that this book makes a worthwhile contribution to the memory of these unique vessels, by resurrecting, albeit only in print, the 'glory days' of the paddle steamers that once operated in United Kingdom waters.

▲ The last British paddle steamer to run scheduled services, as originally intended, the *Lincoln Castle* approaches New Holland pier on 29 June 1977. *Ian Allan Library*

Alongside the Victoria Embankment, the *Tattershall Castle* in the heart of London on 1 May 1976. Originally an art gallery, she is now a thriving pub. Her aft well-deck has since been enclosed to provide more inside seating space.
Kenneth Wightman

The preserved former Clyde paddle steamer *Waverley* during her first visit to the Isle of Wight, at Yarmouth Pier in September 1989. The P. & A. Campbell screw-propelled motor excursion vessel *Balmoral* can be seen in the background. Once owned by Red Funnel, the *Balmoral* is now the *Waverley*'s fleet companion.
David Reed — 10328

The former Humber paddle ferry *Wingfield Castle*, seen prior to her restoration to become part of the Hartlepool Maritime Museum. During this period she was temporarily renamed *Brighton Belle*, in an attempt to cash in on a popular name from the past. *Bettina Rohbrecht*

APPENDICES

1. Paddle steamers engaged in Operation 'Dynamo' — the evacuation of Dunkirk, May-June 1940

			Numbers Rescued	Crossings
Brighton Belle	P. & A. Campbell	sunk 28 May 1940	0	0
Brighton Queen	P. & A. Campbell	sunk 1 June 1940	160	1
Cambria	P. & A. Campbell	renamed *Plinlimmon*	900	1
Crested Eagle	General Steam Navigation Co	sunk 29 May 1940	0	0
Devonia	P. & A. Campbell	sunk 31 May 1940	0	0
Duchess of Fife	Caledonian Steam Packet Co		1,633	4
Eagle III	Williamson-Buchanan	renamed *Oriole*	2,587	5
Emperor of India	Cosens & Co		644	3
Glen Avon	P. & A. Campbell		885	2
Glen Gower	P. & A. Campbell		1,235	2
Golden Eagle	General Steam Navigation Co		1,751	3
Gracie Fields	Red Funnel	sunk 29 May 1940	281	1
Marmion	LNER		745	3
Medway Queen	New Medway Steam Packet Co		2,914	7
Portsdown	Southern Railway		618	1
Princess Elizabeth	Red Funnel		1,673	4
Princess Helena *	Red Funnel		0	1
Queen of Thanet	New Medway Steam Packet Co		2,500	3
Royal Eagle	General Steam Navigation Co		4,015	4
Sandown	Southern Railway		695	2
Solent Queen *	Red Funnel		0	1
Waverley	P. & A. Campbell	renamed *Snaefell*	981	2
Waverley	LNER	sunk 29 May 1940	0	0
Westward Ho	P. & A. Campbell		1,686	3
Whippingham	Southern Railway		2,700	1
		TOTAL	28,603	

Red Funnel's *Duchess of Cornwall*, not listed here, made her way along to Dover in response to the call for relief shipping but was unable to cross the Channel because of fuel problems. Two other Red Funnel vessels (marked *) — *Princess Helena* and *Solent Queen* (1889) — crossed to Dunkirk but, finding no signs of troops on the stretches of beach where they had arrived, returned to Dover empty. During the confusion off the beaches the *Princess Helena* had a minor collision with the Great Western Railway steamer *St Helier*.

2. Paddle steamer literature

The various excursion-steamer operators around the coast of the United Kingdom went to great lengths to promote their businesses by providing mementos of each cruise experience in the form of handbooks, souvenir brochures, guides and magazines.

These documents featured details of the fleets' vessels, maps of the cruise routes, with descriptions of what could be seen on the passing shoreline, and gazetteers of the attractions at the resorts visited. Many had photographs, some had pull-out postcards; some were complimentary, others cost a token sum. Each line produced material specifically intended for the junior passenger.

Among the numerous publications produced were the following:

The Bristol Channel District Guide — Official Handbook of the Marine Excursions by the Steamers of P. & A. Campbell Limited
P. & A. Campbell, prewar, annually (first edition in 1893)

The Eagle Steamer Handbook on the River Thames & Adjacent Coast Resorts
Eagle Line (General Steam Navigation), prewar

The South Coast Guide
Red Funnel Steamers, between the wars, annually to 1936

Day Cruising from the Heart of London
Eagle & Queen Line, prewar

Red Funnel Stuff
Red Funnel Steamers, prewar, annually 1937 to 1939

Sea Cruise
Eagle & Queen Line souvenir magazine, prewar

Seawards
Eagle & Queen Line handbook, prewar

*Now and Then — Eagle & Queen Line Steamers
Illustrated River and Holiday Guide*
Eagle & Queen Line, prewar — priced 6d,
aimed at children

What's What in Shipping
Eagle & Queen Line, prewar and postwar
— contained colour postcards

Clyde Steamers at a Glance by John Marshall
British Railways, 1948
— recognition data with silhouettes,
diagrams and photographs

Red Funnel Steamers
Red Funnel Steamers illustrated brochure,
postwar

Perhaps the most novel give-away produced
was the 'Eagle' Time & Fare Finder and
Weather Forecaster (see illustrations on the
right) issued by General Steam Navigation.
Comprising a folding pair of riveted discs,
it permitted the passenger to dial up the
departure times and fares from different
points along the cruise route or, for different
barometric readings, the kind of weather
that could be expected. When one considers
the kind of weather typically experienced in
a British summer, this latter function of this
piece of merchandising could have been a
deterrent to potential passengers — unless,
of course, they received their gift after they
had boarded!

Also of interest *from*

Ian Allan
PUBLISHING

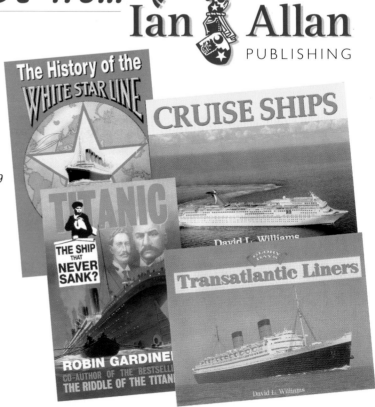